COLD SNAP AS YEARNING

COLDSNAP
as yearning

Robert Vivian

University of Nebraska Press : Lincoln & London

Publication of this book was assisted by
a grant from the Nebraska Arts Council.
Copyright © 2001 by Robert Vivian. All
rights reserved. ⊗ Manufactured in the
United States of America

Library of Congress Cataloging in Publication Data
Vivian, Robert, 1967–
Cold snap as yearning / Robert Vivian.
p. cm.
ISBN 0-8032-4670-6 (cloth : alk. paper)
1. Vivian, Robert, 1967– Homes and
haunts – Nebraska – Omaha. 2. Drama-
tists, American – 20th century – Biogra-
phy. 3. Omaha (Neb.) – Social life and
customs. I. Title.
PS3572.I875 Z474 2001   812'.54—dc21   [B]
00-066631

This book is dedicated to Kay Vivian, Ladette Randolph, Judith Slater, Jay Rush, and Robert Coleman — with deep gratitude and affection for all the wise hours.

Contents

Acknowledgments

Versions of several essays have been published previously:

"Clean Gravel Roads" in *South Dakota Review* 37, 1 (summer 1999):47–53.

"Cold Snap as Yearning" in *Onset Review*

"Mrs. Brock Alive in the World" in *Salt Hill* no. 7 (May 1999):131–36.

"Taxonomy of Garbage" in *Sycamore Review* 11, 2 (June 1999):126–31.

"The Dark Hangnails of God" in *Creative Nonfiction* (forthcoming).

"Conducting Buses" in *Bulb* (forthcoming).

"Light Calling to Other Light" in *Fourth Genre* 2, 1 (2000).

"Empty Cages" in *Salt Hill* (forthcoming).

"Driving to the River" in *River Teeth* (forthcoming).

Rootedness

Hereafter in Fields

THE WAY THE SUN shimmers in the long Nebraska grass just off the highway can make you feel hope again, like there's still time for lovelier, finer things. It hovers in every reed and dust mote, rippling out into the tiny eyes of grain that burn with winter's fire, an ember so small and subtle you know something is burning inside you, too. It's a destination that breaks the spell, that teeters into dread. Dusk can make the fields remote, haunted, the patchwork of all your silent prayers. I drive because I have to. I drive to get where I am going, making the fifty-mile commute between Omaha and Lincoln three days a week. But what about these fields, these grasses? Why do they suggest something about time, about eternity? I'm just another pilgrim in his crude bark boat, making his way across the waters; I'm just another commuter fiddling with the dial. But more and more I wonder what it is to arrive; more and more arrival becomes the thing bequeathed, but not desired.

If only we could keep going, out of harm's way, and take with us only the best part of ourselves; if only we knew why we dream at the wheel or think more clearly while moving down valleys and across rivers. Driving toward the horizon on Interstate 80 can make you feel this. Driving anywhere flat and endless can. It can wear you down to sheer seeing, to that mesh of changing light just over the horizon that blooms like sunflowers drenched in a cut glass vase. Sometimes the clouds above the Nebraska plains contain such towering beauty that you sense the sky is exploding around you in myriad waters, bearing down on you like grace before dying. The grooves of the highway moan, and just outside Lincoln the view north is endless in rolling fields, undulations firm as a roadkill's thigh, a rigor mortis of earth chipped from the moving plates of time.

★ ★ ★

I could never really know these fields anyway; they are meant to be regarded from a distance, because distance is what they are all about, the tan, variegated earth I have grown—begrudgingly—to love. Who lives on this gradual, curving earth anyway? So many people I know curse this Nebraska landscape, saying it is dull and uninspiring, stripped of beauty; one acquaintance I know even called it "the bland aftermath of oblivion." For most of my life I have been in this camp, too, disparaging the state where I grew up because it could not compete with oceans and mountain ranges, soaring skyscrapers and the frenetic pace of urban life. It just sat there outside town like an existential flat tire, devoid of inspiration. Horizon was all there was, a threadbare rim that took you to the edge of nowhere and plunged you deep into sky, leaving your imagination with nothing to cling to. But now I have come to think that even here the landscape can work its way into you by the dreamy process of driving across it, a constant revelation of blue heaven that will never know boundaries, the land beneath it filled to the brim with distance for all comers. Even Nebraska can be a holy place if you are willing to take on the cosmos and yourself, mile by passing mile. I have learned this the slow way, as I learn most things. But see how the earth drops off just beyond the rest stop off Exit 432 on I-80, how the fields to the north define the rough edge of distance like a skinned drum, sounding the hollow notes of forever.

You could taste this north in the wind it brings down, carrying rumors of the pole. You could lose yourself in distance, the metaphysical equivalent of emptying your mind of all worry. Then flatness becomes a virtue, the keen edge of your heart in extended space. I drive between swales cupped like a lover's arm, those secret places we love to kiss and lose ourselves in: valleys that bottom out, humming with fine cirrus of light; the sense of wonder and time that these confer, again and again, driving among them because I am here. You are alive, too, as you read this, and may regard these plains as a boredom to be endured, or as a chance to daydream with your eyes open. But I think the pressure of the plains could change you, the invisible pressure of the land beneath your tires.

Where are the unbroken spaces where the soul can go to be itself? We put so much burden on these fields, we mow them down and cut

4

them up. I want the wide-open spaces where the earth drops off; I want to see the winter fire in the eyes of the hunkered grouse, where the sky moves in a whorl like the drying, spilled ink of the sun. This could sustain you for a lifetime, maybe longer. We can enter the hereafter in fields, moving over the earth, sifting through the fine grains of fire, lighting the sparks that take our bodies home.

I am not the same person after this fifty-mile drive to and from. It doesn't matter who I am in either city, but who I am in between.

I see the brake lights of other cars and the necklace of city lights as I approach Omaha. They hover in a timeless space above the horizon, these jewels, the forethoughts of city planners. They would go on a long time, or as far as the last prefab home, bleak strobes of progress that won't let us down. But progress does let us down, every time. They glow with a threadbare yellow leached of solar nutrients, tired, worn-out, a jaded string of lights that loops around midwestern dreams. Your only defenses against them are the radio and spinning tires. Drive into any city on the plains and you will see them from far away, blinking and hovering like a lasso made of burning embers. But beyond the city limits lie the fields unfolding in countless variations of repose, from the pure potential terror of snow fences banked against the sky to those fields of stubbled corn whose nappy heads ripple as if they as if they were asking the universe a thousand questions at once.

I return to Omaha each time a little tired and fatigued, a cleaned-out feeling the fields work through me mile after mile. The drive gives you nothing you don't already carry inside, waiting only for the appropriate time and space to come forth. It gives you back your thoughts, spread out as if upon a smooth white table. The exact dimensions are not important. They come out only in hints and intimations, nudgings so small they're like a puff of warm air on the back of your neck. The drive can speak to you in barely heard murmurs, or in the wind-hollowed silence of the landscape. What is it they have been trying to tell me all this time? For years it has been like this, a moving whodunit, where I reevaluate my own small life and think of those who make it into my dreams. Then the fields ring me out in their long-grass sieves, soundless harps that play with tiny fingers.

5

I would go into them if I could, wandering knee-high to the bend of a meandering stream. I would look into their tentlike gaze for some brief, fleeting notion of grace. But no doubt this is a fanciful delusion, half-crazed, because what they do best they do at a distance, as a moving panorama, the texture of the earth's body entire and not a particular vale or region where I stand rooted to one spot. I am a temporary voyeur of the moving earth, rolling over it a few times a week, wondering each time at the subtle mysteries of where the land meets the sky, how they meet in changing juxtaposition, and how these work their wonder in fields. Then, sometimes, if I am lucky, I can get the whole feel of it, and I am sucker-punched by grandeur, by my mote-like presence in a world that is meant to knock me to my knees. It has become the difference between hearing and listening, singing and saying, watching and seeing. It's the hereafter in fields, waiting at the edge of every city and small town, beckoning you to lose yourself in contemplation of the land and sky and your brief sojourn between them, joined by the speed of memory.

Boring, wide-open Nebraska, unbroken by drastic change, unfurled paper of an endless map, you have been nudging me more and more insistently toward the beauty of the sky and your own dipped hollows that move like shadows into the thistle of your reeds. I drive across you to get where I'm going. I drive across you to come from where I've been, and you lay it all out before me, a long and ideographed scarf that contains walking pictures and voices.

If your fields wake, we are dead; if you lie still, or move so slowly that even graves cannot hear you, how better for us that we do not know it, that we cannot sense your awful turning, that we cling to the skin of your cheek like mites on a granite face, making our way into the thin creases of your forehead.

I drive because I have to. I drive because I must. But now the drive between Omaha and Lincoln has become the deepest part of my day, the deepest part of my week, the deepest part of my life. The realization has come upon me slowly, like shadows moving out over the fields pulling their slow curtains, giving the threadbare world a dark clarity. I do not know why this is, why certain curvatures of earth should visit this

6

mystery upon me in the declining hours. I suspect it has something to do with memory and how the earth exacts devotion. I am relieved when I cross the Platte River either way, and a little sad. I do not know why this is. Maybe it is the way the winter trees hang near the water's edge like some keening tribe of women whose sorrow would rock me to the core, or the gray way they gather sunlight into the nethermost part of themselves, giving back nothing but deepening shadows and partly reflected light.

I have seen these fields before dawn covered with mist until they become insubstantial in the clouds, haunted by the gravity of their own churning. I could drive eighty, ninety, two hundred years and not know why it is they haunt me so, why it is I keep coming back to them, chastened, wanting to know their secret and the secret of myself. But neither shall be disclosed, not now, not ever. They lie back always just beyond the meaning of time, waiting to come forth in small offerings of silt and clay. Duly, I note my passage across them and come up with little to say, no dirt beneath my nails. This must be why some farmers seem touched with a far away spirit, their blue or brown eyes ineffable for the kinds of sun they see there, and the fields that call to them in dreams like the susurration of inland tides. I drive over the earth but do not penetrate the cusp of it. Only in the glancing, improbable here-after in fields do I sense a reason behind this sloping distance, or how this distance works itself in me, or how they work together to create a yearning for a different kind of life.

Clean Gravel Roads

SOMETIMES AT NIGHT I could hear the gravel road in a wave that came closer, breaking down in darkness to the slow clicks of dwindling rocks, a fading artificial sound, like the earth bottoming out. I'd get out of bed and go to the window. The car or truck would come to a halt, its taillights glowing like soft embers in the dust. Then darkness again, and the two figures in the car would grow motionless and still, or turn to each other slowly. It was always a slow, careful dance, simply executed: maybe the woman touched the back of his head, ruffling dark hair I couldn't see. Maybe he would turn toward her, opening the position of his body. Maybe they would face each other at the same time, car idling or turned off, or melt into a kiss that made their two heads one. In the dark I could never tell; I watched them from the bedroom window.

On a clear night the trees around them and the car itself were oblong in moon shadows, longer than the night itself, fading to those haunted curves only shadows have. In the moon I could just make out their gestures, the outlines of their heads; but no faces, no eyes, no expressions to pin to their secrets. They were too far away. And behind them, leading them to this spot of stolen time in the middle of the night at the gates of a power plant surrounded by heavy pine, the long gravel road wound behind them like the summation of their lives, unraveling piece by piece, leading them here. Two lonely people who were trying to take from the summer night something they didn't have before, solace or sex or the chance to be what they wanted. And I watched them from the window, the night breeze warm on my face. I watched them all summer as they spoke with words I couldn't hear, with faces I couldn't see, in a white gravel darkness that glowed under the moon like hot white rocks fresh from the incinerator of time.

★ ★ ★

The white gravel road was a vein of impermanent passage: it lay like a river frozen in time. I grew up on it, watched its dust devils, its shimmering heat waves, its strange, narrow life that stretched between houses and a field and all that took place there. We rode our bikes on it, walked on it, dreamed above its scar, my brothers, sisters, and I; we came back from rejection on it, strode past it, tried to jump across it in three leaps or less, watched crows gawk their wings on it, saw rabbits pass over it on dainty rocking limbs ready for the sudden bolt into the bushes at the end of the road. We took it to go away and to come back, to put distance between ourselves and home and to get back, pedaling madly over the singing rocks.

One night there was an argument at the end of the road. I heard curses and swinging doors. I heard yelling and sobbing. I tiptoed out of my bed and went to the window. One door to the truck was flung wide open, and a woman was half-walking, half-stumbling across the field of daisies. Her arms were scissoring back and forth in exaggerated precision until she tripped, yelled out a profanity and got up again. I could see that her clothing was haphazard, loose around her rage. She was drunk. Her voice cut the warm night: "You think you can do that to me? You think you can do that to me?"

Behind her in the truck I saw the back of a man's head over a steering wheel. He was clutching it, head bent over it, like he was praying or passed out. For all her stumbling and yelling he was motionless, a part of the truck, no more moved by her curses than a tree stump. I rubbed my eyes and pressed my face against the screen.

They had been there many hours. At first they played soft rock music, and I just watched the back of their heads. They didn't move for a long time, so I went back to bed. But something must have happened in the truck. I continued to watch the drunk woman sway in the moon, her arms going like a slow, awkward pinwheel of supplication, as if she was trying to bring it down to comfort her. She was gesturing to the truck, too, saying hateful, murderous things, and the stump of the man remained prostrate over the steering wheel, inanimate like a hubcap or fender, until suddenly he sprang to life and started the truck, gunning it in reverse and stopping only to close her door. He peeled out in a cloud of dust that rose like smoke above the road as he disappeared into it. I could see his taillights fade into the mist. And the woman sat down in the field and cursed him some more, her shoulders quaking without sound amid the tranquil rasping of crickets.

The woman sat in the field for an hour. She was a part of it like the motes of drifting pollen. She sat stupefied and unyielding, head tall among the daisies. I watched her from the window. She shouldn't have been there, under the moon, where anyone could see her. She stood out in the moonlight. A suspense began to build; I began to look at my fingers on the window sill and hope that when I looked up she'd be gone. I counted off the seconds and closed my eyes. Something bad was going to happen. I couldn't pull myself away and I couldn't go to sleep. It was a reckoning we were headed for, the three of us, between her and the man in the truck and my own secret place high above in the window. But I couldn't tear myself away. The white road lay like a foreboding beyond us, both viewer and sufferer, waiting to carry the cargo of this night away for good.

We knew the truck would come back. We both looked at the white road to see if it was coming. But there were no headlights, no dust yet. We waited another half hour, holding our hearts in that secret place where there is no turning back. I was part of the drama, too: I was watching it take place right before my eyes. I could see enough of her face to notice it was pretty and small, an oval moon rounded by long hair, that she was tiny with her hair in her face. And maybe I wanted to whisper hoarsely into the night, "It's going to be all right. Everything is going to be all right," but that would be a lie and an intrusion. For a part of me wanted to see what would happen, witness the reunion and the malefaction. We sat together in our separate stations, waiting it out for reasons I still don't understand. The night and the road held us both in haunted awareness that something strange, spooky, and perhaps even beautiful was about to happen, that we both would be transported away from our lonely spots in the moonlight. And besides, there was nothing she or I could do. We sat many more minutes alone in our skulls, and I wondered if she had ever been abandoned like that before, if she had lived with this fear all her life, if she expected revenge or forgiveness from the man in the truck, if she wanted to gouge his eyes out or kiss his brow, which I never saw in the dark seclusion of the truck.

When it rained the road turned an oatmeal gray, and tiny puddles of alkaline sat undisturbed in the pockmarked ash. They were bottomless, opaque in their depth. Looking into one was like trying to see through a broad pan of milk.

The road was no more than a quarter mile, curving like a J at the end by the power plant gates. It was magical and still, a lunar landscape surrounded by earth. Most of the rocks were no bigger than a baby's fist, like arrowheads, angular and sharp. They flinted off in a rock fight, cutting the air like crude diamonds that arced in parabolas of near misses and linear curves. They flew like dead meteors in space, without heat or majesty. But when they hit you they sting, and their sharp points feel like the stabs of surprise of sudden cruelty from someone you never thought would hurt you.

When he came back for her it was like her own life approaching, headlights staring hard and bright, with a plume of dust rising like vapors in the wake of his progress. My heart beat fast. He was coming on hard, inevitable. The white road rose behind him like a storm cloud, coming up out of its slumber in an angry thunderhead. The woman continued to sit, watching her fate come on. He was going too fast on the gravel road, but we saw his speed coming direct and merciless, cleaving between us like the difference between the dead and living. She stood up, smoothed her tumbled blouse, and faced her destiny. I continued to watch, hunched over at the window, as the man came to a sliding halt and cut his engine so that the truck went silent and blank, the dust gathering around it in a plume of white mystery before all was still again and the woman walked toward the cab.

I can't get back there again. It seems shorter somehow, less particular of that universal and haunting quality it had for me as a boy. It's just a road. I drive by it once in while and it's not the same. And I can imagine the same desperate parties use it surreptitiously at night, but do the rocks still fly out like missiles from young kids' hands? Do they still fly out in joy and the pleasure to hurt, to hit what they aim for? Do they still hide the white grasshoppers from malevolent feet, clothing them in that sacred synthetic white like a baptism of flour in no man's land?

When I was younger that same white came from another world, it was the perfect reflection of the moon on a warm summer night. Like pieces of bread, it satisfied a deeper, ineffable hunger that was the attraction for walking on it, for seeing our house on it, which seemed so far away that the gravel road was the perfect way to get there, building suspense and appetite even while it fed us. It fed us the same way it fed that man and woman one summer night, giving us something to eat even if we couldn't give it a name. It was home we were looking for, and the white gravel road led us there like nothing ever would again, like a blues song expressing what we miss and can't forget, like the moon itself sustaining in those loaves of our lives the memories of the roads that lead us here or there, or nowhere at all, past the sanctuary or pain of memory where the end is just another reason to keep moving forward over the hushed beds of immutable rock.

She climbed into the truck and threw her arms around the man's immobile shoulders, his head like a potted plant between them. They stayed like that for a long time, a silent tableau of hurt and reconciliation in the lonely whiteness of the road. I watched them from darkness while my brother slept, far off in his dreams. I waited to see what would happen. There was no music now, no intimation of words. Just nothing in a road of nothing.

Now I think they had separate thoughts in words unintelligible to both, so distant in their own heads that even the lasso of the woman's arms was like a punctured life raft between them. Because I could not hear them and they did not move, I believe now they were paralyzed in a crisis where maybe infidelity or sorrow or love was slowly pulling them apart. *What will we do now?* But I don't know. I will never know. But the moon was out, and the white gravel road supported them both in the loneliest of all desolations, human need and abandonment, and I began to grow tired, bored even, waiting. A part of me waited for something dramatic to happen, another scene of yelling and stomping off. But nothing happened: just two people locked in some kind of desperation at the end of the road. She hugged him tight once, twice, ringing his neck for some reaction; and his head just bobbed a little, revolving slightly until he bowed his cheek against the crown of her head, a confirmation that what had ever happened was now behind them. He gently disengaged her arms from around his neck, and she slumped by the window in a heap of spent emotion. He started the truck again, turned on his lights, and as they swung around in an arc of yellow beams, I saw the green eyes of a raccoon flash out of the light and disappear like two bright coins dancing in front of a curtain. The man and the woman left together, slower this time, and the dust rose up again in a haze of release, settling back into place, like a soughing that drifts out of the trees and goes nowhere, and the white gravel road bore upward all its cast-off loaves, vacant and forgotten in the moonlight.

Shooting Churches

W E WALK IN THE WOODS with the older boy, the one with the pellet gun. He has it slung over his shoulder with a strap, as his own long hair falls down across the nape of his neck. We follow him in awe.

"Watch this," he says. He raises the rifle to his shoulder and takes aim at a squirrel's nest. Gently, he squeezes the trigger and suddenly the nest jumps, as if deep within its pocket a young squirrel jumps and frolics. He pumps the rifle again, priming it. He pumps it eight times, the maximum amount. He takes another shot. This time his shot goes awry and glances off the trunk in scrapes of bark. "Here," he says, handing me the gun, "you take a shot." My little brother watches me from the side. He's watching to see what I will do. His eyes are clear windows that have not yet hardened into judgment. They look out with a simple curiosity, a kind of beseeching. I take the gun and hold it. A current of dark energy flows through me. I am holding a bolt of lightning. I take aim just like the older boy, I shoot at a cottonwood branch some distance away. The shot of the pellet is soft, hushed, a discreet *oomph* that cannot be heard even forty feet away. It is the sound of air leaving a bottle. I shoot, and as I fire I pass over into a dark territory that makes me terrible and radiant. I want to shoot something, anything, to prove that I'm dangerous. It's important to feel dangerous. It is that strange admixture of daring, innocence, yearning, and stupidity. I hand back the rifle like a sacred reed; he takes it and gives it to my brother.

We're in a clearing surrounded by brush where no one can see us. A jay cries from the bottom limb of an elder tree. Bart takes the rifle. It's longer than he is. Suddenly I'm alarmed and jealous all at once. He's too young for the weapon, though I do not think this: I think only that he should not take a shot, that he shouldn't have the same opportunity for power that I just had.

He takes the rifle and levels it to his shoulder. He looks miniature compared to the rifle, barely able to get a proper hold of it. But he sets up all the same, as if he's done this all his life.

"Shoot the jay," the older boy whispers, leaning over his shoulder. Bart is stolid and calm, he takes aim at the bird and squeezes off a shot, barely missing the bird by the length of a twig. The jay flies off, angry and calling like a siren of danger in our own hearts. "Not bad," the boy says, and Bart stares at him without smiling. Instead he looks to me, to see what we will do next. But the matter is out of my hands. We will follow the boy wherever he goes. We're too young to escape him. He's almost sixteen, his hair a braided straw mop with a part down the middle. He is tall and thin like an arrow, with the cleft of a scar that runs like a towline from his left jaw to the point of his chin. It is this scar that contains him in confidence and arrogance, the assumption that what he says we will follow — and we automatically do.

We watch as he lights a cigarette and offers it to us. I shake my head quickly and he shrugs. He scatters ash carelessly to the ground, tapping the cigarette like an adult. We stand waiting and watching him, ready to do what he wants. I know we shouldn't be there, but it's too late. Because I am the middle-aged of the group — nine years to Bart's seven — I must follow and lead. Between my brother and the stranger I am a captive of my own uncertainty, both wary of what we are about to do and willing to go further to show that I'm not afraid.

Later, when the events of the day are already settled into the disquiet of the past and we have been punished for what we are about to do, I will wake up in the middle of the night sweating and out of breath, seeing the boy's mocking face as he urges me to shoot my own brother: and in the dream, I take the rifle and turn it on Bart in a slow, liquid movement, aiming at him while he calmly stares back at me and the older boy cackles, his laughter sharp in the staccato of cruelty, mockery, and contempt. I pull the trigger.

As on so many other nights, I wake up panting and out of my mind; asthma causes me to sleep fitfully, to have bad dreams. I go to Bart to see if he's awake, to make sure I'm not alone, knowing he's already been asleep for many hours. I go to his bed and shake him repeatedly, asking, "Bart, are you awake? Are you awake?" until finally he is awake. Then I walk back to my own bed, slip under the covers, and pretend I was never afraid or guilty of anything: I pretend nothing happened, that I acted all right, that even as I shake and tremble it was all just a bad dream, the day and the dream never really happened, and now I can go to sleep.

The pellet gun is polished and oiled, with a walnut stock and fancy etchings in the metal plating. It could be a real rifle, a real gun. Each time the older boy pumps the action beneath the sights, the rifle suddenly becomes something else, hissing with each pump until it's ready to fire.

"There's better targets than this," the boy says, tossing his head to the side to get the hair out of his eyes. He's two heads taller than we are, and in the tiny opening of bushes and trees the sun is going down behind him. We follow him to the edge of the woods without saying anything. We walk across a meadow knee-deep in grass toward the Baptist church. Pines and elms surround it; it is a shard of stained glass dropped in the middle of nowhere. We go to the back of the church. We wait to see what to do next. The older boy squats on his haunches and picks a long shoot of grass to chew in his mouth. "Who wants to take the first shot?" he asks.

I don't want to shoot the church. I want to shoot the church. The church is a space-ship dropped here in the long grass. This is what I think, but I don't say the words because the counterpoint of yes and no, love and hate, fear and longing, the need to tear down and the need to build up are synonymous and one. My knees shake. We shouldn't be here. But I want to be here. The boy is talking to me, but I don't hear what he says. His smirk is a saucer of thin milk. We're at the chain-link fence. There's a small playground out back that is overrun with weeds so that the seesaw and swings are not clear-cut in and of themselves but float in a haze of long grass and dandelions whose heads loll drunkenly in the warm breeze. It's a strange, purple, broken-down church, the kind where the faithful beat their heads against the pews and weep while the preacher sweats bullets from the pulpit and gesticulates wildly into the vast dome above his head. "Repent! Repent!" I imagine the thin, bald preacher screaming while a drooping red and Pentecostal robe strobes fire into the dank atmosphere of the nave.

The boy smiles at me, and I look away. Locusts cry out from hidden pockets in a chorus of heat and sundown. I have heard about Baptists: they bring all the wildness of their spiritual lives with them into church; they're shameless in their demonstrations. They shake the rafters and each other to throttle out sin. But I don't want to be here. I can't retrace the steps that brought us out of the woods into the open. Maybe that's why the boy is grinning and chewing a piece of grass. He's waiting to see who will crack first. The swings teeter slightly, waiting for something to fall.

The boy stands up and pumps the rifle. He shoots out a window. He pumps again and shoots. The tinkle of broken glass falls like tears coming down a cubist painting. The shards sink and disappear into the grass while crude fragments and configurations remain behind. Suddenly the woeful church has changed countenance, it is breaking apart into small parts that multiply in the grass. *Oomph* goes the pellet rifle. The boy is a perfect right angle, with the rifle point-blank at the church. His hair waves behind him lightly, glistens in the sun, it is so soft and fine you could brush it with a doll's comb or put a strand of it in a miniature locket. *Oomph* goes the rifle, and the tinkle continues one pane at a time: he is standing calmly in the sun with all the time in the world. The church will fall one fragment at a time. I am rooted to my spot, I can't move the stone rails of my legs. He has only taken three shots but all his movements are the cool liquid of aftermath. He has done this before, many, many times before, and suddenly I hate him. But the hate is paralyzing; he ventures into the fenced playground. "I want to see what's in here," the boy says. I am frozen by the fence. Bart looks at me and hesitates. Then he follows him.

Together they move into the great shadow of the church, which absorbs them like animals come to rest in the shade. For a moment they are just two dark figures who have lost something in the tall grass. The earnestness of the boy's face usurps any bad intention. He looks worried as he searches along the sidewall of the church. I want to say something. I want to cry out. The cry inside me is like a wind rushing up a hollow place that comes to the abrupt end of a tunnel where the light is sealed up forever.

But I did not say a word. I did not say, "Bart, come back here" or "It's time to go home" or "You shouldn't do that" or even "Why?" I didn't know what it meant, the actions and intentions of other people or the nonaction of myself. I stood still because I didn't know what to do.

The door flew open as two men snatched the boy and my brother. They yanked them by the arms so quickly I did not know what was happening. They thrust them inside the church without rustling or protest. They just disappeared into the interior of the church and left me outside alone and paralyzed at the fence. A man with a tie and horn-rimmed glasses made for me. He looked like a librarian or a teacher. A row of pens dotted his shirt pocket, lined up like bullets from end to end. I bolted from the fence and flew down between the waving grass across the open field. My knees glided over the earth and I heard nothing. I ran away from the sun into the lengthening shadows of my own shape, which grew longer and longer down the steep slope of the sidewalk past the houses I had known all of my life until finally I came panting and breathless to the doorway of the living room where my father was calmly reading the evening paper. He looked up at me expectantly, waiting for me to catch my breath.

It is not clear-cut, this retracing of steps that begins in innocence. We do what we have to do. We move on. We forget. We become someone else. We become ourselves. And what we think we forget is never really gone. We don't have time to remember. We don't have time to forget. You tell me what it means. This is life passing us by slowly, then gaining speed around a corner and then another corner. We go with it. We have no choice. Somehow along the way we put a distance between ourselves and what we did, how we became the people we are today. The distance grows.

One night the smooth, fine hairs of my hands stand up in the dark, I wake up, listen and am afraid. But then I lay back and all is well. The moment has passed. I'm myself again, and I try to convince myself I have all the time in the world. This is my life, I think. It's time for me to live it. And then I fall asleep.

We stride up the long hill toward the clearing where the church is. It's a quarter of a mile away from the house, buried in a lot that suddenly breaks into view. My dad is almost running, his rolled-up sleeves and loosened tie swinging in unison. He has not said a word. He has not looked at me. I sniffle and struggle to keep up with him, trying half-heartedly to invoke some explanation. When I told him what happened he leapt out of his chair with such ferocity that I backed into the wall and knocked into the hallway table. Then he was out the door, and I had to run to catch up with him. Now his arms swing freely, his fists are clenched. The cleft of his chin is clean and determined, he is making a straight line for the church, the granite of his teeth set behind a stare. All I can do is stay behind him. All I can do is follow.

When we come to the church he strides up to the back entrance and pounds heavily on the metal door. His blows land like hammers lined in velvet, thunderous and hollow, echoing out of the quiet meadow. All his reserve has vanished. "Open the goddamned door!" His sudden violence reveals him as someone I did not know before, someone I did not want to know. He is completely out of control. He is not the man who sits at the head of the table eating quietly and telling jokes with a straight face. He is someone else. He lurches from window to window, peering in. He returns to the door and begins to throttle it, to shake it from its hinges, yelling. I grip the fence. When the door finally creaks open he flings it back and rushes inside. Then I am alone again. I wait in the shadow of the church while the sun goes down behind it.

We walk back home, silent and chastened. Our dad's fury has smoldered now, and the silence grows between us. My brother and I are on each side of him. He has not even bothered to reprimand us. Silence is enough for now. He seems weary, as if he has seen all this before. The older boy was detained. No one came for him.

For as long as we live we'll remember the shooting at the church. I stood by and watched; I stood by frozen and unmoving. There would be other acts of vandalism for me, crazy, blood-letting sprees of broken mailboxes and punctured tires. Sometimes the need to destroy is as great as the need to be loved—and neither cancels out the other. They combine in the strange sinking of innocence and the need to test and be tested.

When we first moved into the neighborhood, the very first night, someone shot out our window. It was a solid, middle-class neighborhood, where new houses were built every year. Carefully kept lawns surrounded every house. Maybe the older boy did it? Maybe he was taking revenge on his own privileged life before he even knew what it meant? After the church we saw him around but avoided him. He was always getting into trouble, smoking dope and spray-painting signs. He drove around in a blue Camaro with tinted glass, stereo blaring. He always took the sandy turn at the bottom of the hill in a fishtail, accelerating out of it with smoke and screeching. We were told to never hang around him again.

And now I wonder if the older boy, who is now a man close to forty, ever thinks of the church in the clearing; I wonder if his life is working or falling apart; if he has cut his hair and quit smoking. I wonder if he ever thinks of us as I think of him; if he remembers the shards of glass that fell so quietly they did not make a sound, as the grass took them with the soft, open hands of grace when we thought we were all alone. I wonder if he has made a peace with himself or whether the dark nights of his boyhood have left him stranded somewhere in middle life, staring out a clear window into his own darkness and pain.

Small Rain

SOME RIVER SMELLS or lake smells stay with you forever; just a hint of one of these and we are suddenly thrust back in time where there are no buffers or layers to protect us from our own innocence. They come from everywhere, damp cedar logs in a neighbor's back yard, steam coming off new roofs after rain, all manner of water hiding secret scents in unforeseen places, letting loose the magic of memory and molecule one brief trace at a time.

For me they all lead back to Glen Lake in northern Michigan, where I spent many summers as a boy, with the scent of fresh pine and water running their invisible currents through my grandparents' open windows. I can still see the white curtains of the cabin billowing out into the breeze, then holding flat against the wall only to bloom again in the full-throated arias of breezes. Even now the scent of pine and lake water restore me to my better self, slowing my blood down, making it new again.

I remember my mother keening in the cabin after her mother died, rocking back and forth on the clean, white-linen bed, and the convulsive way she waved me off as I stood confused in the doorway, those same smells mixing water, pine, and death together forever. I left her and walked down to the dock, hurt and rejected, my first confrontation with death a door suddenly closed to me that had been open all my life. The end of the dock seemed to disappear, apparition-like, into a gauze of infinite fog, as I stood at the end of it, looking into the calm water. The water was still, clear, dark glass that lapped quietly on the shore. I became lost in its rhythms, forgetting for a moment the recent death and my mother's rebuke in the small cabin above the lake. You could watch and listen to such water for a long time after being turned away; it could pull you into the currents of other lives still waiting to be mourned. The dock, too, had its own smell, the pungent odors of fish long since caught and cleaned, and algae that grew on the rusty underside of its rigging, with the taste of iron and lake grass in it. Some of the algae would dangle and barely touch the water beneath, grazing it with slow, languorous brush strokes. Then the whole lake was one giant ether you entered slowly as if into a dream chamber.

I can smell the minnow cages bobbing up and down like human shoulders in the lake. I can smell the fish odors of the dock, scales that shine like open tins, and the water that laps at its underside. I can smell the wet sand and almost taste the salty edge of the bank—all of these are smaller than anything I can hold in my hands. Could it be that standing alone at the end of a dock in fog when you're just a kid is enough to commemorate a whole life in smells? Smelling these just once more, I can suddenly see my grandmother laughing again and the slight gap between her two front teeth; I can smell the fabric of her dresses (one faded pattern the color of blood), hear the satisfying sound of cards being shuffled and dealt around the kitchen table, the smooth feel of walnut. They are all just one smell away, and when they come I am always shocked back another magnitude into time. Maybe those smells are a lingering faith in what I thought I had left behind; maybe they connect me again to ghosts who are trying to let me know that the simplicity of death is more beautiful than anything I could ever imagine; that somewhere above me or inside me this shocking reality is every bit worth the wait and the travail, and they are just waiting for me to get through my own endurance and pain. I forgot a long time ago the reason why I'm here, and the smells of the lake bring it back. The dock and all its various smells and odors is the pungency of life in the midst of death. The smell of the lake is enough to bring her back to me, to put me in the center of her laughter, to see again the careless way she held a cigarette, her horsey laugh and smile, the smoke gathering in a fine cirrus above her head, disappearing like a lasso of light rising into the sky.

Sometimes, not very often, even here in Nebraska, I smell something faint and reminiscent of the lake, and it stops me in my tracks. Then I try to recover it, to pinpoint its origins, though each and every time I fail to hold onto its spilled purse of wonders: it is there for a flash only, then gone, like sparrows breaking from a branch in a blur of wings. And I know somewhere inside I am not supposed to keep it—it cannot be preserved—but I try anyway, and this always moves me. Who or what are these renegade scents that tantalize with their haunting baggage, telling me the Michigan cherries are rotting again, the lake exchanging this fullness with its own clean, sudden sweep?

I smelled the lake two days ago in a wet oak branch, though when I picked it up the lake was gone. The lake is always gone. Instead I am stopped in traffic, inching forward at two m.p.h., or standing in a long line at the post office; I am walking out of a supermarket in broad daylight with plastic bags bulging in my hands, and all of it, all of it, leads back to the lake, the circumference and destination of my desires.

You can't pinpoint those smells. You can't summon them at will or wish them into being; you can't even recreate the concatenation of their sequence, the ingredients that send you reeling back to when it all fit together, when you were all together. Just a scent and it's over, leaving you yearning and confused.

In Glen Lake you can wander out the length of many football fields, and the water will turn a deeper band of blue, rising only to your waist. You can see your own feet on the lake bottom, stirring up shells and small stones. You can smell the water even as you move deeper out into it. The simple act of walking into water can be like the restoration of your whole life, a deep calm and mystery, and maybe this is why we come here. Smells move around you the way they always have, a wood-burning stove back in the cabin, the faint smell of coal and ashes on the beach. Or on the slender shore where another dead fish is gathering its panoply of flies, its one staring eye a bottomless black hole. Far away in Nebraska, I can only report that these smells are real and circling an invisible river that lets them loose just once in a while when I least expect them. Back here, the smells of the lake reveal themselves from their secret hiding places only at privileged moments, leaving me stunned all over again in the knowledge that everything I have ever wished for is still waiting in a patch of wet bark, mist in the sycamore trees, runoff trickling by in the sudden, quicksilver lightning scent of the lake after it rains.

Cold Snap as Yearning

THE BRANCHES WAVE slightly as the white sky blows cold and arctic across the ends of the field, beyond to where the plains roll out into nothing. I see everything: these waving sticks holding a roughage of green—a few buds of life—that taken together add up into knobs that multiply like the bumps on an old man's forehead. The blanked-out sky high above them: whiter than bone in all directions. The more I look, the more other worlds come out, exploding out of the whiteness of my seeing into other greens and other whitenesses, other stars I did not count before. Concentrating on these bulbs and this sky and my own frozen breath, I am magnified to a still point in a world without sound and movement, except the wind and the branches and what my arms do as they hold my body rigid in the snow.

I am eight years old and have buried myself under fitzer bushes during a harsh Nebraska cold snap.

Until you have buried yourself under bushes in a Nebraska cold snap—with just a vast and cutting edge of the sky open and forever—you do not know what silence is: not the absence of sound alone (because here sound is still around you, though closer somehow to its sources), but a clear stripping away of any falseness or echo, or any movement that is beyond your life because you are beyond it, lying face-up in the snow where all eternity lives wide and separate in the sky. The wind blows over you because you are finally part of the earth—the part that cannot be spared from the ancient contradictions of wind and silence.

I went out in the storm to watch. I needed to know what it felt like—at the absurd temperature of thirty degrees below zero—to lie down still and soft where the snow fell lightly across my arms and legs, to burrow down into the cold white powder and watch and listen. Cold fronts come too seldom when you're eight; instead they come out of your dreams or ambush you suddenly when you thought you had lived the winter life faithfully, seeing the frost and ice curl up at the corners of windows and the beautiful blankness beyond them, negating the streets and sidewalks and everything in their path.

School had been canceled. The city shut down to its minimum capacities, nothing moved on the road outside our house, no lone figure made its way anywhere except in rooms similar to ours, shuffling like us in wool socks and slippers, like us simultaneously trapped and free inside our homes. The radio was on, announcing shut-downs. The Czech Society would not meet at five o'clock; the girls' choir at Duchesne Academy would reschedule practice for Thursday the fifteenth, weather permitting—call for further details. The litany was endless, and very delicious. How could you argue with the perfection of a cold snap? On a day like this you stay inside and sleep in, read a book, or otherwise laze about the house, looking at pictures or soaking in the bathtub. Everything else is frozen and dead. It is a brief and necessary quarantine.

I went to the window and looked out. Nothing moved that the wind didn't move first, all was locked deep within itself, smoothed over like a rib cage lost in a freezer.

Something tugged at me, something beyond the windows and the snug world of afghan and woolen socks, drawing me out. I begged my mother to let me go outside for twenty minutes, *just twenty minutes!*— and after haggling with her, stomping my feet, shedding false bitter tears of hurt and disappointment, I finally wore her down: it would be better for her to get me out of her hair for even a few minutes than to be cooped up with a fuming malcontent, mooning at her in doorways. So she let me go with a sigh and shake of her head, somewhere between weariness and anger, scolding me to dress appropriately and be back in twenty minutes.

And I did. I dressed like an astronaut preparing for another world of ice and wind where nothing, surely, lived, except me and those bar-

25

ren sun-forsaken rocks that lit grayly on the dark side of the planet. Each sock and boot had to fit perfectly, each layer of ski mask and scarf wrapped around my head until only my eyes showed in a turban of wool and polyurethane.

"Twenty minutes," she said, and I nodded, my whole body of a piece like one solid cork.

I went out the garage and, where the door lifted, met a foot of snow shelved perfectly crystalline and pure, as cut off from its natural bent as I was. I stared at it long enough to notice its perfect glazed angle, the weightlessness of its glide, like a different kind of wave caught midsurge before it crested, arched where the pearl white of drift was severed by the metal dungeon of the garage door. Humbled, I stepped clean over it before the door closed behind me without a sound except the pulling groan and settle of its chain.

I trudge across an open field that is endless for its blankness, each rabbit hole or declivity settled over in one smooth curve. My breath blossoms raggedly in the air, a ring of ice forming where my mouth is covered by wool.

The earth lifts before me like a great veil of white holding up its immaculate vision, a table set with fine white linen as far as I can see, except the trees that rattle and shake their brittle arms. I am a speck on the board, a tiny insect making its way over a blown anthill. At eight I am looking for God, or what passes for divinity in blown snow and nothingness. I walk on and on, the crunch of my boots magnified in the cold. Where I am going is difficult to say. Each boot comes down in a place not touched before. I move off into another distance. I notice my breathing, the buffeted feel of my body against the cold. The wind holds me, then pushes against me from all directions, as I sway like a staggerer lost to visions of wagons going by. The world has shut down and thrown away the keys. The earth has stopped pretending, the owls have stepped over the last bones of the field mice. I am marching toward eternity in a suburban neighborhood that is no longer well kept and friendly: it is an outpost winnowed out of the cold wind, plopped randomly here in the snow in the middle of the plains.

★ ★ ★

I know where I am going. There is a power plant in a park across the street from our house. It is surrounded with bushes and trees on all sides; in summer we race around it, we make caves and shelters in its foliage. Now it has been abandoned on the edge of the world.

In a certain spot away from the chain-link gate, you are safe from the wind underneath the bushes, so I crawl there as the prickly branches tug and poke at my winter suit. I am shimmying my way on my stomach, burrowing down into the ground and clearing a spot of snow. It is tight work, and the more I struggle the more the bush seems to jab at me with hidden barbs. With my boots I snowplow the powder backward toward the opening until it piles up outside the entrance. By thrashing and swimming in the snow I create a dugout that fits perfectly around my body and the surrounding branches. Then, after struggling and breaking my way in for six minutes, the shelter is complete. I roll over carefully like a deep sea diver to see what I can see. I look up at the sky and see nothing but white everywhere, white so white the rest of the world is blotted out, blank, unspecific as a free fall through clouds. A branch tugs and bobs in the wind with those tiny bulbs of green, and I hold my breath and wait. And wait. And still wait. A fine mist blows across my face on its way to disappearing. The tiny snowflakes melt into my ski mask.

How often do we know we are alone, not the alone of self-pity and pathos, but the shattering alone in a place that is placeless, in a world beyond our knowing? I am eight years old and know nothing, and it takes my breath away; and then something is revealed to me in the cusp of cold wind through branches, though I cannot say what it is. Silence and cold and wind blowing, the *via negativa* of coming briefly to the end of my chain, not straining at all in felt emotion: the zero where I become nothing in watching the blanked-out sky, the whisper of the wind through branches that are the difference between seeing and being.

Then it is over.

I am hauled back to the world of the living by one tiny, invisible thread, I am conscious again, I crave cocoa, my wool mittens are chafing at the wrist, I squirm and discover that this much snow and this

27

much cold is suddenly unbearable: whatever spell I was under is broken, it's over now, time to go home, dry my things by the fire, try to remember what just happened, though it will take twenty years to make any kind of sense of it, one moment of eternity where I stood outside time and gazed at the sky and found it unbearably peaceful because I was not myself or anyone in the snow but a witness to what I still do not have the words to say. I say goodbye to all that. I heard the monosyllabic moan of nature and found there was a place for all of it, my breathing, those branches, the cold and the snow, the sky beyond them white in every molecule, that all of these are still valid now and forever though the meaning is not clear. In fact there is no meaning but emptiness, and this emptiness saves me for one split second of my life that will carry me for years — has carried me, in fact, to this very sentence at the beginning of the new millennium.

What I want to say (or whisper) is that you do not matter, and neither do I; but that is neither an issue nor an obstacle but a starting place in the snow under branches as a young boy who knows nothing learns something in the brush of a drift that falls gently, almost imperceptibly, over the mouth of his ski mask down the passageway into his larynx, where he coughs the snow gently and mist rises out to the open sky.

I did not think these things at the moment; I think them now.

When I come back in, tired and sleepy from the exertions in the snow, my mother opens the door for me and asks about my trip.

"I buried myself in the snow," I say. She nods and unbuttons my hood.

"Do you want some cocoa?" she asks. Her cocoa is homemade, a sublime, chocolate powder with flecks of white. I sway on my legs like a sailor.

"Yes," I say. She goes upstairs and I take off my boots, one at a time. They drip and melt on the concrete floor of the storage room. I hang my coat and ski mask on the clothesline with wooden pegs; they are abnormally thin and long, pulled down by the weight of their melting. I want to curl up in a corner and sleep like a dog. The wind moans outside. My brothers and sisters run around upstairs; I hear their feet pounding the floor like boars breaking out from the brush. My mother's voice calls out sharply, and the stampeding stops. I wait for something, anything, but nothing comes. The furnace hums, my clothes drip, my hands droop over my knees. Whatever I was looking for was lost long ago. Whatever I find is gone the moment I find it. Whatever I love is with me always.

Dreams I Had of Hiding

I

N THE APPLE-GLOW of early summer, you could hide all day under fitzer bushes, foraging for a clean place in the world. You could burrow down and in, the sun filtering through prickly branches, sifting the light and drifting it down to a mellow kind of dusk before the real one came. Then you could watch the people walk by, you could in all your nervousness and stillness take in their arms and legs and torsos, or the tanned calves of pretty girls that seemed to go on forever. You could watch the simple life of a sleepy neighborhood unfold before you. In the bushes, too, you could cry your heart out, look at old comic books, experiment with fire, or pretend you would never go home again, not ever, because here you were safe and real, safer and more real than you were in your own bed at night. But even then you knew that for the rest of your life you would need a place for hiding, any place; you would need a corner, room, or bush where the deep roots of time could sink their way in down to the nethermost, suck up the reasons and the causes — even if they did not make sense — to go on and out again into the business of the world, renewed. These would do for an interval. For we must have hiding, places to lick our wounds, if only for a little while. I am troubled by this, and moved. We must have hiding, places where we can drop all pretenses not to just be ourselves but to dissolve into something else. We must have hiding, because we are not private people after all; we are in our own dreams the pull of the same ocean, waves that break and crest together. We can't avoid our human obligations. We must have hiding, because it is only here, away from the processes of society and people-forming, that the divine kernel of ourselves is lit and stays glowing among the hypocrisies of the day; we hide because we need to, to let the fragile wick catch fire, burn innermost, keep going, keep going.

II

Where do you hide? The silverbacked gorilla at Henry Doorly Zoo in Omaha won't turn around to look at us; his great head is like the back of a foothill, covered in the dark earth of ashes. He has been sitting like this, Buddha-like, for hours. People tap on the Plexiglas, taunt him with yells and jokes and funny faces, unconscious of their cruelty. He has been stared at all day, every day, for years now. Flies come down from the rafters to nip at his crown where a bald spot is forming, a small pond of gunboat gray, a bald bored into and scrutinized by every human observer, but he doesn't turn, even as a kid calls him a worthless overgrown monkey and people laugh.

In shafts of sunlight that only zoos seem to have, the woefulness of the gorilla's caged life is on public display: great piles of shit are spread over the floor as if in some mapped-out archipelago, islands of waste that connect him to his own confinement. They sit around him as if to say, "We knew you when you were free. We knew you when you bedded down on the misty hillside, opened your mouth to yawn, when your strong arms were waving precursors to your sleep." But now his arms are crossed, his back sapped of all caring. This is public misery of a special kind.

A zookeeper could come in and tap him on the shoulder and he would not turn; someone could confront him with his own shit, throw it at him, prod him with a stick, hoot, call him names from five feet away or less, toss a chair at him, go right up and sniff his backside, imitate the behavior of another gorilla; but he would not turn, not now or at any other time, no matter how much this paying crowd demands to see his face. He refuses to give us the false titillation of fun-house terror and stalking, to play his transparent part of rage and fury; he refuses *to perform* for us. But a zoo is not a place for hiding or private mercies. He must play the role he was assigned by capture. That's why he's here in the first place—to be gawked at, resigned to the stares of people who do not deserve to see him like this. Still, he tries to hide in public, or at least turn away from the glare, from the human faces that come in and out each day, faces that never change, that cannot change, faces that afflict him with staring, the scald of public regard. He cannot avoid them forever.

At night when the crowds have left, and the sounds of the zoo resume their nocturnal stirrings, coos of pigeons and staccato hoots
from the bird house, I hope he can turn around if he wants, wander up
to the glass, tap on it with his great knuckles, and then pound away for
all that he is worth, to rage at the dull mirror that always shows him
himself and the bland, undifferentiated crowd. I hope that at least in
darkness he can hide for a few hours, be his true self, wander out under
the stars in the cool night air of sweet oblivion, sniffing and cocking
his ears for the distant call of his ancestors.

III

In the tunnel of bushes, a texture of woven branches, you could also
begin to imagine the deaths of others and the death of yourself. You
could lie down deep in the heart of a quiet country where no one knew
where you were, close your eyes, and hear the church bells tolling as if
they were made of falling water, water that took a long time to reach
the ground. This was hiding, too, the death knell behind all hiding,
hiding that rang you up to a kind of troubled sleep. If no one knew
where you were, and you closed your eyes against the heat and light of
the day, were you not almost dead already? Then you became all ears,
waiting against time for the small music of the world that revealed
itself only in that precious state; you lay there because you had to,
something was calling, a deep message sung by grasshoppers sawing
their small bones from tall grasses. You became the buzzing of flies,
waving branches. You became a wheat field in the rain. In this dream
of hiding, there were no false moves committed in sleep. You listened.
You had to listen. The earth itself became a kind of audience.

IV

Once my brothers and I heard on a transistor radio that in a secluded
city park not far away from us, a man had killed two girls with a broken arrow shaft, an asthmatic murderer who gulped for air and tried
to wash himself of his victims' blood in an empty car wash. He gasped
for air, they said, he gasped mightily for air like a dog who had been
shot through the lung. We heard this on our bikes on a dirt road two
miles from where the killings took place; we hightailed it out of there,

keeping our eyes peeled for the Arrow Killer, who might jump out of hiding to attack us. I pictured bloodshot eyes and curly black hair dripping with sweat. I pictured a man whose skin was a pale cast of green, cadaverous, fishlike, a haunted predator from the depths. We rode home as fast as we could. When we got there we learned the killer was in my sister's grade, a fifteen-year-old freshman named Samson. He carried a bottle of pills wherever he went. He wore plaid shirts, buttoned collars. He said "hi" to you in the hallway. He was quiet, she said, shy.

The radio told us he was hiding in bushes before he jumped the girls; he stabbed each of them eighteen times. One of the girls was last heard asking, "What did I do? What did I do?" Both of them died later at the hospital, and the killer was caught astride his bicycle, shirtless, pedaling out of town on a lonely access road. His jeans were speckled with blood. He was trying to hide again, to run away from what he had done.

I do not want to see what he saw. I do not want this kind of hiding to be sanctioned by power, the ability to ambush and overcome. I do not want this hiding to haunt me with its dark potential or veil; I want it only to be that place we come to when our resources are tapped, and there's not anything inside us but the great inner ear left for listening and quiet. But I can't turn away from this hiding, or the hiding of others who lie in wait to kill or to hurt. This is the dual nature of all hiding, the bedding down of deer and the disturbed young man who must take out his revenge on others and on himself. Because there is blood in hiding, too, or the potential of blood. I cannot hide like I used to as a boy. That hiding is gone and finished forever. I cannot be a small animal anymore, peering up through interstices of woven light. This hiding must stay with me only in memory, in dreams of innocence and maybe a deeper receptivity to mortal truth, now woebegone, now part of the changing past, that taught me just a little about grace and the potential of filtered light to heal something I cannot name. Because only there would the world come to a teetering stop, wobble on its axis in the great heal-all of space into a kind of focus, that you had the rest of your life to figure out.

I want to know what it meant.

I think it meant I couldn't come this way again, it was a temporary gift to see my way through trouble. This and only this is what hiding has come to mean: that the Samsons of this world, with their anguished breathing and sudden flights are hiding, too, they are meant to hide inside the awful shears of their own minds so that they can break forth in darkness. My dreams of hiding had to admit a darker spectrum if those slain girls were to have any peace at all in that place we call memory; they had to be full of arrow shafts as well as clean small stones. Because hiding is a tightrope we walk between darkness and light. We hide to get away and we hide to plot revenge. Only we know what we hope to find in hiding, how we reconfigure the possibilities of desire and longing. I try to hide to get in touch with listening. Why do you hide, and what has it gotten you? Are you under the net for a reason you cannot name? Is that place a sanctuary or a reckoning? The deeper sounds are concealed from us, and in hiding we can hear them. But we can also find a deeper darkness, too, the bushes allowed you to stare with impunity at things and people you lusted after.

V

Now they are dragging the muddy Missouri for the missing man who was last seen gambling on a casino boat, his pockets full of ticket stubs; now the tomcat across the alley is looking for a place to hide, slinking along the wall to escape notice, his figure disappearing in flowing cursive. Now I think that hiding is full of sorrow, sanctuary, and the possibilities of evil, too, deep aches, the closet beloved of all parts; now I think we need hiding so that one day finally we do not have to hide anymore, from others or from ourselves, even if we have to disappear to do it.

The dreams I had of hiding hint that I wanted to turn myself inside out, listen for a while without interruption, go deeper, deeper. I hid away to listen. And this is what I heard, the music—manifold desire—that can last a lifetime: small birds and wind in the trees, spokes of bicycles flapping with playing cards in their spokes, the chink-chink of lawn sprinklers, distant voices, ordinary sounds, summer sounds. And I heard—or thought I heard—the deep tide of my own blood rasping in my ears as if for the first time, the tide that takes us back and takes

34

us forward. I listened for the one sound or word that would make all the difference (though I cannot say now what it was). Like all children, once I was the quiet instrument the branches played through in music and light, music in light. The rest of hiding was simply a before and after of the briefly sustained note, the note that sang of eternity under a canopy of branches, branches that shifted in the breeze and brought the light down in a rustle of fine whispers, music beyond seeing and out of this world.

Anthem

WHEN MY GRANDFATHER DIED, he was wearing a white hospital gown in a room he shared with strangers. The last time I saw him, he was moving his long skinny legs back and forth, sashaying to the rhythm of some invisible pain. No one said much, or made small talk that was both absurd and woefully inadequate. "We're all here, Dad," my own father said softly. There was nothing else to say; the stroke had rendered my grandfather mute and restless. Even in bed he kept moving his limbs, his mouth open all the time in shocked wonder. We were all there, my four brothers and sisters and I, and my parents, who looked grim and ashen. The orange walls of the hospital gave his dying a color, one I would learn to associate with death, a goldfish color. I remember hearing moaning from other rooms, the clatter of metal instruments. Everything seemed to be falling apart around us, as we stood still at the center of the deepest kind of mystery.

We had come all the way out from Omaha to Muskegon, Michigan, to see him, and he was withering away slowly, losing his mind piece by piece. I thought of bone yards, I thought of mules. I thought he was a boy playing an old man, or an old man pretending to be a boy. There was something slightly obscene about his dying, like we were watching something we shouldn't. Time was all wrong, horribly mixed up; the bores of his nose were filigreed with stray hairs that moved as he moved. If only he would stop rocking back and forth, I thought then, though I didn't exactly think it. I wanted to close his mouth; I wanted to gently take the yellow and crumbling rows of his smoked-stained teeth and sew them shut in the calm certainty of death or sleep. But that is good for nothing. His mouth was the wrong, renegade pain that howled without sound, that took away his dignity without his full knowledge or consent. He was screaming to let the world out, one silent ribbon at a time.

We stood around him in a half-circle. His dying was not specific enough, not encompassing of that region of his life that contained the grouse feathers of his youth or the mystery of Lake Superior. He should not have died there when his heart and soul were up north in the Upper Peninsula of Michigan where he grew up. I will go to the end of my life believing this. The site of his death was a mistake somehow, a horrible, metaphysical screw-up. He was a country boy, after all, a true child of the woods. Both his parents died in a flu epidemic in the early 1900s, and he and his six brothers and sisters were forced to go south to Detroit to work in the auto factories. I don't think he ever recovered from this, though in truth I didn't know him that well. I only know that he used to keep all of his life savings in the trunk of his Buick, that he distrusted doctors and dentists, and that he once took out his own abscessed tooth with a buck knife and a few shots of Jack Daniels. I only know that he lived the best way he knew how, with a fourth-grade education and a gift for fixing things. But I wish he could have died where he wanted, near a campfire maybe, or in the middle of the woods next to the bleached rib cage of a deer.

I think if I could ask him now where he would want to end, if he could do it all over again, he would turn his hawklike face to the magnetic north. I don't think he would answer right away, or that his answer could be found only in words. Maybe I write this because I am named after him, and my mother says I am more like him than any of my brothers and sisters or any of our cousins. He was gentle and stubborn and set in his routines and patterns—his odd gifts to me. He liked to drink and smoke and have a good time, and his afternoon tea had to be made in just a certain way or he would have none of it. He was a pain in the ass to live with, and he was extravagant when he had money, spending it on others and on himself until it was gone. He was and always will be my one human link to the world of nature, to the mysterious lives of trees and the furtive movements of small animals. They made some kind of sense to him, he understood their strange moods and errands. I think about his death a lot, almost every week, and I wonder what he is trying to say to me from the other side. Because the words he uses (they are out there somewhere) are like smooth stones in a river. They breathe of the far American north and the way the winds change there.

If only I could have laid a freshly caught walleye on his chest, or given him one of his own rolled cigarettes; if only I could have recreated a gesture in memory that would have made his passing more peaceful; if only any of us could properly love our dying in the right way and give them some emblem from the direct roots of their lives, then maybe death would always be a beautiful, holy transference from this world to the next. Instead, I gave him my innocence and horror, and a choking desire to run away. I gave him nothing, not even pity, because I didn't know how. None of us did. He was already moving beyond us, into the burning past where the memory of his life was a warning that none of us could ignore because it licked at the insides of our own mortality. He looked through us without seeing us, as if we weren't there. But we were there, and slowly he wasn't, and a part of me now wants to see what he saw, to go with him into that furnace; but more likely I am fooling myself, and even now would recoil from his dying face rather than take his hand and hold on.

Later we walked out into the sun, and I broke down in the parking lot. My dad put his arms around me and told me everything was going to be okay. I was ten years old. And what haunts me now is that I was the only one who cried; I was the one who couldn't keep it inside, I was the weak one. I try to understand why none of my four brothers and sisters cried, why my parents didn't cry; this is an unfair accusation, but I still feel compelled to make it. We have never talked about his dying since that moment in the parking lot. Maybe because it is too difficult, maybe because it is too painful. This causes me a fair amount of uneasiness, even anger, and I give part of it vent here. What do we do with the dying, other than to let them go? But I can't let him go, and I don't think I ever will. My grandfather was not a great man; he did not have a great career or make very much money, and sometimes he was difficult to live with. But he worked hard in this life, too hard, and his death was not a noble one. I am trying to understand this now, in my early thirties, and what haunts me most is the betrayal of his memory to the margins of a peculiar kind of oblivion, one that is sentimentalized and negated by mortal fear, and the vague uneasiness, finally, of failure. I believe there is more to him than we know, that he lived his hard life for a reason we must try to infer, even if we can never come up with any answers. I sense him everywhere in my everyday life, even more than the presence of my own parents. Maybe it's the way I turn a door knob, or regard a certain kind of breeze; maybe it's my own penchant for pressed shirts and chocolate, the profound pleasure of simple things. I, too, am set in my ways, distrustful of institutional power. Where do these traits go if they aren't found in his children and grandchildren? How are they transformed into the present moment?

I knew standing in the parking lot that I must never forget this moment, or what I had just seen. I had to carry it with me through the years, let it grow of its own accord into something I could use and recognize. I would be called to make an offering some time. My own dad rarely talks about his own upbringing. But once my mother told me his dad was in a bar one night when an acquaintance told him how he'd seen my dad's name in the paper for football; he told my grandfather what a good player my dad was, how hard he ran. My grandfather was surprised; he didn't know his own son was such a good athlete, that other people actually knew his name, went to see him play. From then on he saw every game my dad played in and stood at the very top of the stadium, smoking his unfiltered Camels. He just needed a small surprise to wake him up. He just needed a hint, a murmur that his own quiet son was maybe something special. I'm beginning to believe that this is the way for some fathers and sons, that they connect through disconnect; that the path is never straight, that respect is earned sideways, from the tongue of a stranger. This is how it was for them, how it is for us. We see each other only at a late and flickering hour, when the simplest things turn mysterious and the familiar becomes extraordinary. My dad's dad never had to say he was sorry for missing so much of his son's life; he simply started showing up, lending his silent presence to the importance of certain moments. Riverlike, he moved in fluidly where before there was absence; and I know my own taciturn father sensed the difference, that he played a little harder, ran a little faster. I don't know what it's like between a mother and her daughters. But in my family, fathers and sons share the deepest connections in silence, moving into mysterious grooves, lingering over fires and whiskey. Part of me wishes there was another way. But this is not for me to judge. Inertia and the untold stories of blood bind me silent and steadfast in the presence of my own father, as he was with his.

When I think of seeing my grandfather dying, with my brothers and sisters beside me, I am chilled into knowing that his death is who we will someday be at the absolute hour, trying not to flinch in the face of it. Maybe my tears were a betrayal of this hidden pact, the stoicism that keeps the world's ship from sinking. Everything we knew about him could not conceal this truth: that the last fire is real, that it warps the one we love into another creature, that we must love him or her even in the midst of transformation and find something to sing about when the trap doors of the body swing away and bottom out into the dark, empty pit of redemption.

There's another story I've been wanting to tell for years, a story like all stories based partly on magic and partly on myth. This one is about a boy who was leading a team of horses across a frozen lake in northern Michigan, and how, suddenly, the ice cracked in the middle of the lake and the team fell in, horse by tethered horse. They thrashed there like mythical beasts out of Horace. The boy lay down on the ice and crawled toward them, as their crazy eyeballs went thundering and wet in their plastered skulls. He crawled toward them and started to talk to them in a low voice, wooing them almost, saying that he would take care of them, that he would never leave them, that everything would be all right. Slowly, surely, delicately, he extricated them from the black, seething water like some boyish version of an equine midwife: first one came out, shining and fully formed, then another and another. They came out in a miraculous sheen of horseflesh. These must have felt like tiny studs of paradise come down to shock him with hope. He spoke to them the whole time, he whispered into their huge, slippery ears like a lover of all their kind. Later there would be compromises, disappointments, hard times. But then there was only clarity and purpose in a land still unspoiled by broken dreams. There was only this silent, stern love.

This is what you need to hold on to for the rest of your life; this is what will lend the hard times beauty and mystery so that even in dying far away from here, in a place you never wanted to come to, the horses and ice of your boyhood would come back to restore you. Even though you were out of your mind at the end, I will remember the horses for you. I will sing of it to my own sons and daughters, to those who haven't yet been born. And this is all I have to give you now—your own memories refracted through the lens of a terrible death, and the child you made there at the foot of the bed, the one they gave your name to, the one who will not forget you.

Women

Mrs. Brock Alive in the World

I

OR YEARS I have been watching the same middle-aged woman pick up trash in the street and start to talk to it. She wears black horn-rimmed glasses and a cheap red wind-breaker, and her brown hair is severely cut in the style of a military recruit. Once her hair was long and stringy, constantly drooping over her face; but one day, after I had not seen her for months, she came around again, her hair buzzed, cropped close, the transformation of a wild woman into a disciplined searcher. Her hair has been in this style ever since. She is thinner now, too, beyond slender. Her wiry build is even more reduced, a bony wraith in her uniform of wind-breaker, polyester pants, and gummy Converse tennis shoes. Every time I see her she is thinner somehow, more angular, as if her body is being strained through some infernal sieve that leaves only the muscle and sinew clinging to her bones. Her skin is pulled tight over her skull, and I can see even from my window the pattern of cracks and wrinkles around her eyes.

She does not smile. She does not look around. She does not stroll or take her time. She is all business, making her rounds, addressing her chosen ones in the street. Milk cartons, branches, a ruler speckled with paint — it does not matter: her choices seem arbitrary, but after closer observation she always chooses pieces of a certain forlorn quality, and then they are the focus of all her concentration and endearments, as she stops, picks up, inspects, pulls closer as if to nibble, sometimes sniffs, and begins her long, sweet, low harangues, her face going stern, then tender, then twisted with rebuke, as if she is finally asking of these objects just to be themselves, to stop pretending to be something else, right now, to knock off these silly charades, that she is disappointed in them but still holds out hope; then how sorry she is that it has not worked out—and how dare they pretend to be something they're not and talk back at her. Then she flings them away in disgust, even stomping on them occasionally. It's always a full revolution of hope and rejection, as if some seed in the object she holds suddenly goes sour, and it's time for the rage and the bitterness. Her demonstration is one of utter heartfelt regret, for in each and every case some strange, secret pact is violated—the resistance of the found to her small fingers—and she must continue her search for another object strobing out from the hidden colors of the street. She is looking for the final piece that will complete the feverish picture in her head, the picture inspired in the bright, mad chambers of her mind where everything has the potential to bridge the gaps between significance, a concatenation of signs. Then it is on to the next item, the next search for hope and interest, the next cycle of lost and found.

Like all of us she is looking for order in a chaotic world—and her search is desperate and hard-won, like all of ours. But something is different with her, though I can't say what it is. It is not her mental condition or the ferocity of her searches: it is not quite her small, manlike body or the demons at her door. Something else is eating at her. She is looking for peace and not finding it. She is combing the ground for worthiness. She is going down into the street itself for deliverance, and the street is beating her, one piece at a time. It's a hopeless war of attrition, and it's taking its toll on her mind and body. I call her Mrs. Brock because one day, suddenly, that's who she was to me. Her name suggested itself to me, and I have thought of her so ever since. And Mrs. Brock is doing the best she can in a strange and troubling world, an odd woman on the verge of madness. She is searching the underbelly of things to get at their meaning, past the muck and the beetles. Once in a while she carries a Styrofoam cup of coffee, and this cheers me beyond reason, as if this small gift of comfort takes the edge off her searches. She needs coffee, too. She needs the hot, brown liquid, too, the caffeine kick, the stuff of early morning hope.

Whatever she is looking for, I hope she finds it. I hope one day I will look up from my desk and see Mrs. Brock prostrate on the walk and beaming, holding the one true thing that shatters the prison in her head, as the light pours in from all directions, and she kneels humbled before the cleansing force, the light that will heal the dark wounds in

her heart. But this is romantic and melodramatic. Mrs. Brock is alone
in the world. Her search is doomed to failure. And the gears of her
body are long past the straining point, her buzzed, knobby head just
a symptom of her losing battle with the refuse of other lives.

II

I try to imagine this small corner of the world without Mrs. Brock, this
midtown in Omaha with old houses bunched together; I try to imagine these streets unhaunted, without the beggar figure living out the
peculiar, harrowing dream of a life gone wrong, as she searches for
something in other people's garbage. Maybe she is picking up where
we left off, sifting through the stuff we throw away. Maybe she is a dark
reminder of what could happen to any of us, a shard of crooked glass
that reflects us warped and out of whack. I try to see what she sees,
feel the rough edges of her pieces of bark and soggy cardboard lids. I
try to get at the small grains of meaning in the scattered trash of the
street, the bleary pictures of magazine models torn from their pages
and landing chaotically, still smiling, ripped apart in the bushes. I try
to see what Mrs. Brock sees. But I can't do it. I can't see what she sees.
I can only guess what she's looking for and why. I can't see the reasons
behind her searches and seizures.

One day I passed her in the street. For one whole block we were approaching each other—and my heart jumped, turned over in my chest.
I was nervous and piqued, excited even. I kept watching her come on,
I kept looking at her face. She was scanning the ground, picking up
items, throwing them away. What would we do when we finally faced
each other? Would she smile at me? Would she rake my face with her
hands? We got closer and closer, as if drawn by some invisible string.
I watched her face. She did not look at me. Within ten feet of each
other I started to smile, a big, broad, artificial smile hoping to please,
hoping to convey my harmlessness and understanding that we were
in this together, I was looking for things too, I knew what she was
about. She walked by me without a word, stone-faced. I wasn't there.
She smelled of dank weeds and the peculiar sweetness of a cellar. She
smelled like childhood. I stood stock-still, looking after her, and this
woman I had seen so often from the periphery of my sight suddenly
came into terrible focus: Mrs. Brock took me home. And suddenly I

remembered things I didn't want to remember, a hot summer night in the attic of our house, frightened because the crickets would not stop screaming—and I felt suffocated, my heart began to beat faster and faster, and I felt Mrs. Brock and me pass through each other, as if in our brief passing we changed places, and the world became purple, swirling, and confused in a tangle of hurt and strangeness that wouldn't go away, because this life as we live it is full of pain and hope, even in the drifting, scattered wreckage of what we throw out and leave behind.

III

Mrs. Brock is 5′4″, with a fine Roman nose and gray, hawklike eyes. I saw her hands once, and they look scuffed up and rough—an artist's hands—with chewed-down fingernails and blue, powerful veins like steel cables under her skin. Her teeth are yellow. Her buzzed head seems a bit too large for her body, and she emanates an intelligence gone haywire—and completely inside. She is the kind of sturdy, rugged individual who could sleep outside or in, defecate in an alley squatting, or eat her lunch standing up or on the go; I could picture her at an archaeological dig working the rubble for ten hours or building a fire in the woods and cleaning the bores of a rifle. Every step she takes seems purposeful, to the point, no wasted effort in her gaunt, stringy body. She never smiles. She never laughs. Her guttural voice seems half-German, the harsh sounds that escape her throat like a train screeching to a halt.

These are the things I can picture her doing:

1. hauling a raft

2. cutting wood

3. teaching about the bone structure of a marsupial

4. canoeing in a rain forest.

These are the things I cannot picture her doing:

1. going to a wedding

2. wearing a party dress

3. smiling for pictures

4. weeping at a movie.

By such scenarios and antiscenarios I weave her narrative, conjuring her life among the rubble of a working-class neighborhood, scouring the streets for meaning and never finding it. Like clockwork, she is disappointed and moves on; like time itself she is burrowing into the ultimate marrow of things and coming back to the land of the sane and living to garble her secrets in half-gestures of despair, muttered warnings, warbled oaths, improbable curses. For from her mouth profanities pour like a fountain: the "fuck-back of fuck-all" and the "shit-heads staring from piss-holes." Her lexicon is rich with the mad profanities of the dislocated and downtrodden, the arcing trajectory of rage and disappointment. She has a tidewater of filth in her mouth, and the tide is always rising, spilling out in shrieks and terrible promises, half-heard down the block. Like some injured and dangerous bird from another exotic, faraway place, her songs and cries are out of place in this neighborhood, as if she has landed here against her will, looking for the special leaves of her native land.

IV

Now she is here, bigger than life: from my window I can see her pause to scrutinize a Ho-Ho wrapper, holding it so close to her face she is breathing it. She mutters something, whimpers a little, throws it away, takes two steps, stops, looks back, and shakes her fist.

Who are you, Mrs. Brock? Where have you come from? She is shuffling off again, shoulders slumped, no coffee this morning. Will she ever catch a break? Or is it all going to come tumbling down on her, the weeks, the months, the years? I wish she would grow her hair out; I wish she would go somewhere quiet and rest. She appalls me, she interests me. I feel sorry for her, she makes me smile, she makes me mad. But already she is gone, beyond my view; already she is looking for the next hopeful thing, the next promise of scattered things. Why are you here, Mrs. Brock? Where did you come from? A late summer wind rings the trees without that heavy layer of heat, in the small whispers of decline. I will go my whole life without knowing who she is, without knowing why she haunts me. I will go my whole life without understanding who she is or what people are—why some of us are different, why some of us are broken.

Horse-Woman

THIS IS ALL I remember of the horse-woman, a brief recognition in a pane of glass as she walked by in the snow. I saw the head of a horse in a woman's shawl, a white affair that was tied delicately around the horse's brow. It was a strange sight, discomfiting: it was exactly like a Marc Chagall painting come alive, as the head of the horse and her wide open eyes glanced at me from the papery slopes of the shawl. I suddenly wanted to hold onto this shawl for all I was worth, as you would the reins of a galloping horse or the hair of a lover. I wanted to touch it as you would a nun's habit, or the long train of a beautiful bride.

I was sitting in a coffee house arrayed with twelve-foot windows. It was snowing in swirls, feathers of delicate lace. The city seemed lost in some deep contemplation of itself, buildings separate in the secret habitation of themselves. I was alone. I stared outside. I saw the head of the horse and the woman's body and her brief glance at me before she resumed headlong into the wind. Imagine the long ridge of the horse's jaw and the thin fingers that held the shawl in place and you will see the composite figure who has come to haunt me for no reason; the slender figure and the hosed calves revealed just below the knee in a gray dress; the long, tapering folds of the shawl itself, the perforations like gauze, the pattern of a winter kind of flower, the filigree, the ripples. The horse-woman walked into a dream and there I was, hypnotized in front of a huge bay window, agape at the sudden, inexplicable need of horses. If only she had been a horse or a woman, not both, I could have wrestled with the meaning of her appearance; if only she would stay still in my imagination like a rock or a leaf I could have touched the shawl and held on.

If I had wanted, I could have run that horse-woman down and fed her a cube of sugar from my hand. Instead, I took the huge, terrified eyes as my own. I saw the horse-woman in the middle of the day in the middle of downtown Omaha, and it scared me. I looked around. No one else had seen her. No one else had taken the imaginary reins away from me, the shush in the ear and the great furl of tongue. I got up and pressed my face sideways to the glass. I followed the horse-woman from a distance, and she never looked back, not once, as the snow moved in valleys around her. I could almost taste the glass. My breath formed an aurora of frost. Maybe my imagination had played tricks on me; maybe I was seeing things. After all, I had been staring outside for minutes. I was lost between worlds; I thought there was no way she would get through the day without being discovered or even shot, hauled into a circus tent kicking and screaming. What I wouldn't have done to help her somehow, direct her fate. I sat down, a little shaken. I picked up my book. I put it down. What had I seen? I laid my head in the alcove of my arms. I closed my eyes. I said a brief prayer.

But the horse-woman was already gone. I would say this prayer later; I would make it up when it was too late. I was fooling myself. When would my half-gestures, even in thought, finally amount to something? I looked outside again, searching for her visage. In the whited-out sky and the few tall buildings, I saw the strobe light of a transmission tower. It throbbed like pain at the top of a hotel. The horse-woman was my secret, an inviolate gift given only once. I would not see her again. The terrified eyes would haunt me only later. Parable of the absurd, it was not given to me to know what it meant: all I could do was describe it. My mind was playing tricks on me. Something like hunger moved in my blood, though I wasn't hungry for food. Somewhere the hay was buried under a foot of snow. Somewhere it was late and the wind loosed a cacophony over the fields. There was nowhere to settle down and sleep that was not exposed somehow, though the need for wandering would not go away. Horse-woman had abandoned her shawl outside of the city limits, and one by one, her limbs took on the qualities of a horse, as her black belly burst the seams of her dress, which blew away to a thicket or the slanted woefulness of a wire fence.

51

II

I never saw a woman with the head of a horse. What I saw was this: a young woman not dressed for the weather, clutching her shawl into the oncoming wind. Her dress was gray, and she had on an inconsequential jacket—and the shawl. She held it around her head like a long, tapering blanket that wanted to fly away. She did look into the coffee shop and our eyes did meet; but her look was far off and glancing as mine locked in on her eyes, which did not see me as much as they grazed me like the porcelain clash of dishes. She was looking for something else, and her face was long and thin—horsey—and her eyes were huge, close to bulging, that kind of staring that suggests terror. I watched her walk by. I did look after her; and what I saw was that her right leg just below the knee was bleeding. She was bleeding and wandering the city. That explained the wide-open look in her face. And I never saw her again. I was given such a sight and I had to do something with it; I brushed up against haunting or terror and I had to react. Her face was so long and horse-like, her eyes so wide that for a moment I was convinced she was somewhere running in a field, though only in her head; she wasn't really a woman at all. Her real life was miles away, perhaps even two thousand years ago; she was one of the most beautiful horses I have ever seen. Only she wasn't a horse. I had no intention at the time of turning her into something she was not; after all, she was a woman, a human being, and maybe she was just shocked by the cold and her lack of preparation for it. Maybe it just took her breath away. And maybe that blood was a laughable accident she was hobbling to get away from, searching for haven somewhere down the street.

For the rest of the day the wind blew hard, and the activity of the streets was muted, and all the hard edges and bright angles of the corners and lights were blunted and softened. The popular, usual bridges between fact and fantasy collapsed. Chagall weather. I saw a woman with the head of a horse, and it frightened me and moved me into shivers and shame. I fell down into a deep well of dread. I thought I did not know myself at all, and I thought suddenly that the world was a subtle, mysterious, and shocking place, that horses could have shawls and women could be horses.

III

We took our breath together in that moment and held it fast. We were connected by the possibility of gulping air. We shared suspended breath and surprise, shock, pity, and rife awareness; dreams, anguish, and terror; flicker of recognition, scurry, and defeat; the possibility of blood, limping; the separation was never meant to be hers, the separation between her crucial head and the rest of her body.

I made a barn for her in my mind, one that had a stall and a fancy bureau, hay and a four-poster bed. She neighed and spoke in Italian. We didn't share a thing. We were tied by wanting the same things: clean water and a warm place to sleep. Children came round to touch her; we went to the movies together. She ate popcorn with her left hand. It was an absurd affair. We parted as friends and she ended up walking down streets for the rest of her life, holding the shawl around her head, clutching her secret, nibbling on leafy garbage, and sleeping on grates. Her body never knew where the horse's head had came from; she was a freak of nature. She died with foam oozing out of her mouth. Maybe she was discovered by a policeman on horseback, and the police horse backed away from her body, spooked and prancing. It took them three days to come to grips with their find. Maybe they released a statement to the press, TV crews came to town, all anyone could talk about in their living rooms was the horse-woman and her thin figure and teeth as big as dominoes. It was a sensation. Talk show hosts joked about her in monologues. She became a banality, a postmortem freak show. She was swallowed up in a shriek of meaninglessness, tabloids, news magazines, five o'clock leads. She entered the *Guinness Book of World Records*, she was desacralized. She died alone and inconsolable, holding her shawl. Grave robbers stole her head one night from the cemetery and tried to sell it on the black market. But without the horse-woman's body it was just another equine head; after much looking and threats, they threw the horse-woman's head into a rich man's pool, where it bobbed up and down like a log before he discovered it one morning.

I imagine the horse-woman's birth before she came into all this horror. The doctor drops his forceps, the nurses scream, and the mother is delirious. Somewhere she learned to dress and carry herself like a

53

lady. She was old-fashioned and shy. Very possibly the horse-woman was a terrific dancer, but we will never know now. Now she is just a legend and something to hold onto.

When I saw the horse-woman, maybe I should have followed her and coaxed her into an alley; maybe I should have kissed her forehead and put a bag over her head; maybe I should have snuffed out her life as painlessly and as quickly as I could. Maybe I missed an opportunity to do the right, merciful thing. Maybe I should have fetched a bandage or a bag of oats. I was wrong to think I somehow owned her, wrong even to think that I could help her. We were separated by more than glass. Seeing her got in the way. All I can do now is to try to never take her for granted. It will be difficult, though I cannot see the exact disproportions. I pass by people who are hurting everyday. It's important to know that. I will try to remind myself of that each day. No one is a horse or an antelope. Life is strange. We could be anything, or nothing at all. I have never petted a horse. I don't know what they do with their hooves. The people I love are sleeping as I write this. It is a new year. There is a bloom of aching where I saw the horse-woman. It is tiny, invisible, and broaches no explanation. I carry it with me wherever I go. For no reason that I can discern, everyone I meet carries this aching, too. They carry it like millet seed in their pockets, to feed pigeons or horses. And who knows what single seed will give these creatures courage in the face of death? Who knows what encounter means, or the strange likeness of horses?

The Taxonomy of Garbage

I

A FEW MONTHS AGO I clipped a story from the paper about a woman obsessed with garbage, one who classified it according to her own peculiar needs. She was crushed to death by a garbage truck while she was inspecting the week's load at her own apartment building, her body pinned between the maws of the compactor and the Dumpster's cage, squeezed harder and harder until she lost consciousness and her ribs, sternum, and spinal column were broken and scattered in the small pond of her body. She was a tiny sixty-year-old woman who wore a turbanlike hat that spun around in rainbow colors, like a honeycomb of ascending light, winding up to take off. The article noted how the driver had wept upon discovering her lifeless body and his own unwitting part in her death. Police said he was beyond consolation. "What have I done? What have I done?" he kept asking. He was not issued a ticket. It was the woman's fault for putting herself at risk, for snooping around the Dumpster while he was just doing his job.

The article stated that the city of Omaha would not institute any new policies: this was a bizarre and tragic event, something no one could foresee (an obsession with garbage, a one-woman band); it gravely confirmed the need for caution around trash containers and garbage trucks, the necessity of putting distance between oneself and trash removal. This was the official version, bereft of any deep content—bereft, even, of bereavement itself.

I put this clipping in the center of the refrigerator door. I stared at it. I looked at it each day. It faded in and out of my psyche. She looked out from the refrigerator, caught in the nether world of white on white. I looked at the woman's picture, the exotic hat, the huge glasses,

55

the drawn face without a smile, the vacant eyes that went on forever from the small grains of ink. People talked about her for a while. How shocking, how strange. Did you hear about the woman obsessed with garbage? Did you hear she took it into her home? It was the kind of story reserved for gentle wackos, souls adrift in the wreckage of life, odd loners who were destined to haunt our alleys and sidewalks on evenings when the rest of us were safely inside. Implicit in most comments was the prejudice that really, in a way, she got what was coming to her—not that she deserved to be crushed to death, for God's sake, but that . . . well, one just doesn't *do* that sort of thing: root around in garbage, collect bottle caps. Not if one wants people to mourn one's death. She and her bizarre story lingered for awhile, and then quietly slipped into oblivion where she properly belonged, out of touch and beyond any concrete cause and effect.

But gradually I came to see her in my dreams, and she began to insinuate herself in the nooks and crannies of trash bags, the seams of rotten lettuce. I began to look for her in corner drugstores, hear her whisper in a made-up voice: Don't throw it away, don't throw it away. For a time she followed me everywhere I went. She follows me still. She reconfigured the potential for strangeness (garbage! of all things), the desolate humps of each week's waste lined up on the sidewalks in growing significance. Where did it all end up, after all? It was a secret I could no longer avoid, this vagabond woman and her ridiculous hat, at least not at the risk of dismissing a God-given mission. Her death and story operated in the subterrain of consciousness, somewhere down and out where a picture becomes a story and a story becomes a life. Did she maybe have a point? Was she on to something? Did I know her somehow? Had I seen her before? What did it mean, this collecting of garbage? Was she trying to tell us something we could not quite make out? The things we throw away are legion, they bob in unseen oceans at our feet, moving in the wake of our disregard. Who among us would sort through it, strive to arrive at sense and meaning? Who among us is prepared to sift through the archaeology of our dreams and urges, the sprint to the 7-11, the aching need for Pepsi and condoms?

Neighbors say she was quiet and polite, saintly even; that she was regular in her habits of walking around the neighborhood on her strange errands. She had a Ph.D. in sociology from Columbia. She

worked on her dissertation for twelve years. She did not teach. She
lived alone. They said she returned each day with bulging plastic bags,
that she must have been in great shape for her age. Once she gently
accosted her neighbor for indiscriminately throwing a plastic milk carton in with the rest of his trash. Could she take it off his hands and put
it with her pile where it belonged? Baffled, he gave way. I can see him
holding her off at arm's length, the odd exchange, the surprised look
on his face, the gentle offering. His sleeves rolled up, he looks from
milk carton to her to carton again. He gives it to her. He closes the
door of his apartment a bit flummoxed. What the hell did I do to her
anyway? Single-handedly, she turned her building into conscientious
recyclers—some of her neighbors even went so far as to save choice
bits and pieces for her strange collections: suddenly they saw their own
garbage as something significant and special, even preordained.

Now I think I need to know her more than ever, when what I buy and
consume is not enough, and I hear my neighbor's TV blaring. Now I
think I know what she was after, at least the region of her endeavors,
the implications of her need: I look one last time at the things I discard,
just for a moment, to hold up into the light and ask (it is a profound
question), What did I hope to get from you? Where did you come from
and where will you end up? We are dislocated together, you and I, jar
of empty peanut butter, pears, beans, baggie of sloshed bread. I am
going to get rid of you, shed you from my life. You served your purpose
well, you served no purpose at all, you were the lever of my need that
left me wanting after all. Good-bye. We will not meet again.

II

I said, "Because I'm feeling magnanimous, I'm going to get you a paper towel."
—overheard

The article said her small apartment was immaculate and spare: it was
also strewn with garbage in neat piles, arranged like eggs by size and
substance. They were families, groups of lost children, bottles and
boxes, plastic caps and aerosol cans. Dog tags marked the bundles like
exotic ores, B-1 through X-D2. Sheer inertia and humility had brought
them to her door. Somehow she kept it all from smelling and stinking

out the place: the bundles were small, discrete affairs, dainty as biscuits reserved for a Sunday brunch. She cleaned her chosen ones, washing them with soap and water carefully and rinsing them of their own decay. They slumped serenely side by side by side, earmarked for the next incarnation of their lives. Here the consumer meets her long-lost impulse buy, the quick snatch from the convenience store, thrown away in haste and vague disgust. They were all here: the late night hours, the TV binges, the damned search for love in convenience. She was remaking a world from scratch, shelving it away with loving hands, the true orphans of the street.

I picture her looking out her own apartment window at night, alone with her goodies, going over the day's haul and counting each bag. I picture the slow rummaging of her hands, the rustling sounds, the sudden pause and mental note, the joy of the newly discovered prize, singled out for all her care and attention. For she was careful, we must remember that: this was not an arbitrary exercise in rescue, this was the real deal, a movement toward order and peace.

But surely a spark had crackled long ago, snapped the delicate cables of her mind, threw the whole network of cognition into a serious funk. Twelve years is a long time to work on a dissertation—it's a long time to work on anything. Sometimes the price to be paid is measured not in years but in sanity. We go down and never come up. We get blue in the face, we get scattered and never achieve again the bounty of clarity. Who ever said the crazy must be killers or lunatics tearing their hair out? Sometimes they live next door; sometimes the words *crazy* and *sane* merge into one, until there is no distinction between them, between a compulsive need to shave a pencil each morning in a clean office and an unrestrainable urge to walk around looking for that precious scrap of garbage that will make all the difference. Garbage had become her holiness, her lost gift. That was all. Maybe she was working on a theory of who we are by what we throw away, what this says about us as a society or an individual with hang-ups for plastic spoons. Who knows. It was so strange and breathtaking and sad, this intelligent woman's obsession with garbage. It seemed a postmortem declaration of yearning in a castaway world, a stab of kinship with the victims of our convenience: Q-tips, Kleenex, soda bottles, *People* magazine, egg cartons, water bottles, gum wrappers, life savers. Reading about her each day was like confronting a possibility for human beings I had not considered before, her effort to classify our garbage. She was after something. She was rooting around in egg cartons, pizza boxes, sour milk for a reason, like she was working backward piece by piece toward some revelation. She refused to take garbage lightly, to throw away a bag of rotten fruit and be done with it. Instead she hunkered down and went willingly into stench itself, hand-picking her own private society. What a shock to know someone was keeping count, noticing and caring what we blithely discard.

I do not imagine she talked much of her late vocation, of her fidelity to garbage. All of it—her story, her death, the garbage man, her lids and bags—resist final explanation.

III

Where does the garbage man go from here? Where would *you* go? He crushed an old woman to death, heard the gears turn over as on any other day, grinding and pressing trash into grids and plates, horizons of waste. The driver must see her like a ghost around each corner, between each bleep of his truck backing up, her hat like a cone of color, her body thin as the tail of a possum. In fact, he must see her everywhere, feel her crushed body in his hands. He must hate her and love her for changing his life, for causing him to question his own livelihood. Garbage was his job, not hers. He took it to the stinking dump where the birds collect in hundreds. He took the stink home with him. And in those dark alleys before dawn, when most people are asleep, he interrupts their dreams with the high, metallic whine of the giant cage that shakes and trembles in the neighborhood. He's the rude wake-up call, the loud slam of routine. Maybe he has said, What do you want from me, lady? over and over again. Maybe he has not said anything at all. But every morning it is dark before dawn, and he must haul the garbage away. He must take our waste and hidden sorrows and brief pleasures, even desperation, and drive it all away from where most people live. This is his job. This is what he does. No one escapes the recycling of the universe. And the woman in the funny hat goes with him everywhere, counting the trash, trying to fit all of it into a cosmological pattern, the multitudes of waste and where it finally ends up, in hills we dare not imagine.

Reading the Mail

I N READING THE MAIL, she becomes another person, someone even older and wiser than her ninety-four years; her brow furrows like fire beetling across a field of grass, eyelids moving in patient fervor. The cards and letters are from a long time ago and from right now, in the rocking present. The pages lift in her ancient fingers like dry leaves rustled by the wind, and the wooden floor is solid beneath her feet. This is how she lives her life now, one card or letter at a time; the script bleeds like the water or air her flesh is heir to. I know there is life here, secret life, words like a wind or wave that can never stay still as long as she lives.

Picture an open kitchen, sunlight pouring in; picture a woman at the end of her life sitting at a table, shoulders stooped in a blue cardigan, eyelids moving. Wind shakes the trees outside, dapples the ideographs of leaves and branches in a net around her head. There is dust in the corner. The air smells of old letters, sounds of the sustained, mellow ring of the letter opener whose frequency is higher up than hearing. This could be the end of the world for her, or just the beginning. Small spidery veins map out the latitude of her fingers, blue smoke and purple lattice, soft and aged around the fingertips, touching the hem of memory. *Dear Katherine, Dear Kate* the letters begin.

Sometimes, not often, this is the way it was. I dropped off her mail in the outer slats of her apartment door, and once in a while (only occasionally because usually I was too quick in getting away), I ended up in her living room, bearing witness to her rite. She called me in from the land of irresponsibility, where I had myself and only myself to worry about. I saw her read the mail just a few times in all the time

I knew her. I watched her read the mail because, looking back now, I had no choice; it was destiny or fate that still makes no sense, that renders me motionless and still in memory as I watch her comb through the delicate grains of a lifetime. What she needed I could not give her, the simultaneity of other human voices, yet she gave me so much where time and space collapsed in the odd significance of reading what people sent her. Sometimes I noticed the return addresses: Hastings, Nebraska; Salt Lake City; decaled peaches from Georgia. They were from all over the place, postcards from Europe, the hasty scrawls and exclamation points of places she would never visit. I noticed a line or two, the quality of the script, but only now do I attach any significance to them. I was merely a part of it. She was a woman who outlived entire neighborhoods and farms, world wars, crises; she raised other people's children, lived on Social Security and the kindness of others, and now all that they had to give her, those who were still living or remembered her, were communiqués from the other side of the earth or just across the county line.

Who knew that she would end up here, alone, taking in more than she could possibly carry; who knew that her life would be this harrowing, this shocking, this beautiful, before the final fire? We need to drop down, lose ourselves in reading as she did, consume these letters from each other, the ones written from the core of ourselves. This is what she had to teach me. This is what I have had to learn, dumbstruck and slow though I am.

She was losing strength every day, she was dying, and she still believed in the fundamental goodness of people; she still believed in following through and doing the right thing no matter how much time or effort it required. She still lived in a clean apartment, mended her own clothes, remembered everyone's birthday, believed in America. Once I carried her laundry to the washroom downstairs; she showed me how to let the water run almost tub full before you put the clothes in. She preferred to hang-dry her clothes inside because the dryer was hard on clothes. Tiny things, but full of the gestures of caring. She took the cap of detergent, emptied it, and then rinsed it out again in this same water, the iridescences beginning to bloom and scatter in the cycle. She told me this was the way to do the wash. I remember the small ruby ring snug around her left "wedding finger," the slow care of her wet hand, the fingers sure in their touch. Suddenly her sense of time was my time, her rhythms my rhythms. We waited it out together. She told me about growing up on a farm, her large immigrant Czech family, her father's penchant for boot making and the clay pipe he was never without. It stuck there, she said, like a slat in a windmill.

She told me how hard it was to be a farmer, how desperately she wanted to get away, how the bitter nights could be, how tricky it was to work the coal stoves, how much she loved her father and ten brothers and sisters, how most of them were dead now, how they divided up the farm a long time ago. She told me all kinds of things that seem from a different planet, where the weather could make or break you, not merely inconvenience you. Her stories had the imprimatur of the biblical, so caught up were they with flood and wind, cornstalks and rain. And I might ask her now, gently, what it is I am supposed to do with this special knowledge; how I am supposed to give it coherence or meaning in the world we now live in. I might ask her what place this story might have beside others less selfless and full of excess, including my own. I could ask her so many things, things I have no right to ask, things that only compound the mystery and growing horror. Because toward the end of our friendship, she began to live almost entirely in her memory. She began to see the world from her different, peculiar angle, the one time had gobbled up long ago. She knew who the president was, what year it was; but all other relevant and timely reference points began to fall by the wayside. The pace of modern life left her far behind in her cloistered rooms, shut off in infirmity and old age. She lived for the mail. She posted letters to points all over the country. Her handwriting became like earthworms sliding off the table. The script could barely hold itself together, so shaken was it by tremor and palsy.

And then one day she called me over, had me sit down, and told me while shaking that thieves, thieves she knew because she had raised them from the crib, kept sneaking into her apartment at night and re-arranging her furniture and heirlooms just to spook her, just to drive her out of her mind. They would take a brush or piece of crystal and then disappear for days at a time. They slipped through keyholes and air vents, phantoms of young female shapes who mocked her in her own living room. Later she would find her valuables in another place, under her bed or in the oven. There was no rhyme or reason to their fun-house games—except that they no longer wanted her to live alone and be self-sufficient. "They're trying to drive me out," she kept saying. No one believed her stories. Her friends accused her of being ungrateful.

How could I tell her I didn't believe her? How could I undermine her simple faith in me? She was asking me to bear witness to her suffering, to see what she saw, to take in the outrage and the malevolent spirits. The lines around her face had softened, gone limp; her whole body seemed to sag and slacken, as if the sudden impossibility of peace had rendered her flesh just a bag to cover her frayed spirit, the sad light in her eyes. Her skin became doughy, ravaged by strange sightings. She was slowly falling away to madness—and it was taking the dignity of her old age, her very body, right along with it. I told her I believed her. I made sure her windows were secure. I checked the door, and rechecked it. I told her that she was safe in her own home, that if anything should bother her, she could call me. I told her everything was going to work out. That the truth was on her side. We would lock out these ghosts together. She had the locks changed three times, four. But it was no use. They kept coming back.

Later they just took her away. She vanished overnight. I never spoke to or saw her again. They took her to live with relatives, as if thirty years in the same apartment never took place. I didn't want to know this. I didn't want to get drawn in. I didn't want to know that I wasn't ready for what she had to teach me. Maybe I'll never be ready. She read the mail as if her life depended on it, as of course it did. There, in the kitchen, while I sat some across from her and across time, she went through the diaphanous scarves of memory, big band music, tiny buds of another world shaking around her head. She was shrunken, medi-eval almost, her white hair matted in a net, her hands at a distance from her body in the posture of a much younger woman, those hands so much younger than her face, hands that had wiped away the feces of children not her own, rocked them to sleep, applied bandages, dispensed home remedies, canned peaches. These hands were at odds

with the other withered parts of her; they held her up in a kind of reverie; they cut her off from final decrepitude, gave her the dignity she
had made of her life.

I choose to remember her like this. There in that small dining space
near a bay window her life made sense, could be put into some kind
of order or meaning. There she was in control of her own destiny, the
destiny contoured by the words of others. And reading the mail, some
mail, can be like this; it can be this same dropping down, this same
collision of different worlds, where reverie and destiny meet. I think
she was fully alive in the content of these letters. I think they gave her
solace in a way nothing else quite did. I think reading the mail for her
was what she had come to after all, the ordinary, extraordinary, mun-
dane stories of others where she was the sole audience, the diviner of
fate. What else did she have to live for then, day after day?

She is reading now before me. I can't see the color of her eyes. Her
glasses are perched on the bridge of her nose; the fire continues to
burn toward the outer edges of memory, pulling the words back into
context, rippling the smoke that feeds the mind's wind. You can't predict the arrangement of meaning. She is reading in the last, invisible
archway of her body's slope and magic. The letter is translucent in
her fingers, yellow like a candle flame. This is how we go around the
world, one word and letter at a time. Gather the small mesh around
your shoulders. Let the words go on forever. The room is still and quiet.
Hum of the silver letter opener. Bone chip of hot tea. This is what we
come to. This is how we run away. They will never take you away in
the space between your reading and your memory; they will never take
away the vast rooms, lakes, and midwestern skies of your heart's affliction. You are safe here, and troubled. The afternoon is long. You
will take a nap. The letters in your dreams tumble into one. I needed
to tell you this. Someday we will be together. Someday we will know
what the end is together.

Deliverance of Dolls

MY GRANDMOTHER LIVES in a small house booby-trapped with dolls. They flail out from every corner or tabletop like gangs of straw-haired, chestnutted wonders, pliable bodies of sawdust and rigid bodices of ceramic; plastic curves and canvas booty, black dolls, white dolls, yellow dolls—pint-size beauties the length of your forearm and buxom floppies with banana fingers and tresses like Wagnerian sopranos. Not just dolls either: toy soldiers, figurines, puppets missing their strings, Kewpies, stuffed animals, miniature action figures, rocking horses, cardboard cutouts, pop-up books. She is a woman who lives among legions of the second-hand and the misbegotten, smoothing their brows with a plastic comb.

At eighty-seven, and without having once driven in her life, she still makes her flea-market rounds, walking or taking the bus, setting up her stall among the other buyers and sellers in the industrial part of Muskegon, Michigan. She goes in for the elephant brooch and the glowing-skeleton watch, 7-Up salt-and-pepper shakers. Once she bought a miniature brace of Spanish swords for fifty cents and sold them later that day for fifty dollars. They were no longer than toothpicks, with keen edges that could cut through meat. Every Fourth of July, her birthday, she dresses up as a kaleidoscopic, improbable Statue of Liberty, setting off bottle rockets and sparklers with her great-grandchildren. She still bowls, still lives in the house on Morton Street where my dad grew up with five siblings and one bathroom; still does crossword puzzles and word games; still makes dandelion wine in the bathtub; still visits her living brothers and sisters (all of whom were born in Hungary whereas she was born in Michigan); still walks everywhere, still plays practical jokes, still bakes, still feeds the squirrels outside her window. She is as indefatigable as the moon. None of this would be remarkable were it not for the fact that she has led a very hard life of work and sacrifice, finishing school in the second grade to go to work in the factories, smelting foundries, and paper mills, only to later raise six children and nurse her husband at the end of his life. But she has never struck me as an uneducated person, for she is painstaking with her words and fast with numbers, she is ruthless in a bargain, and rarely does she let fly a half-baked judgment on anything; if you ask her, for example, what it was like to work in a factory for most of her life, she will look through you to the other side to something hard and adamantine. She will say something like "You get through it" and leave it at that. It is as if through all the decades of toil and struggle mere pettiness and self-aggrandizement have been pressed out of her forever, as if in her own body the seeds of malefaction and ordinary human bitterness have been crushed and dissolved. She is noble to the core.

Last summer I watched as she lifted her dress like a little girl and waded in a stream near where we were vacationing as a family. "Where's Grandma?" someone asked, and I looked over the heavily forested patio and there she was, playing in the water all by herself, looking for stones on the streambed. So freakishly young and old did she look that for a moment I did not recognize her. She was focused on the streambed floor, stepping daintily and bending with surprising suppleness, looking for a smooth, black obsidian stone. She looked like a stocky white bird that had landed suddenly, her plumage fantastic in the sudden clearing of light.

She was looking in a stream for the one stone that would make all the difference, the subtle stuff of magnetism. She was murmuring to herself. Yes, to the streambed, no, no. Whatever it was, she found it and put it in her pocket, and her white hair looked like loose gossamer in the sun and she looked impossibly wild, and I wanted to go down there and see her and at the same time keep my distance; to touch her on the arm or shoulder might shock me into death or another life I was not ready for; to touch her, that strange craze for living might strike me, too, and then I would be looking for stones or leaves with that same quirkiness of spirit, with those same careful steps on the shifting, slippery sand.

* * *

Back to the house where she has already gathered another army. They are motionless now, but at night alone she can talk to them and they will respond. They speak in words we can't hear, and once in a while she combs their hair and buttons their starched coats or blouses. Once in a while, they talk back and plead to her to save them. And maybe she combs them because no one else will; and maybe she talks to them because no one else knows the words. If the phone rings, first it must be gotten to, and she makes her way around the columns of things that rise above her. The house is a health hazard and a great tinder-box waiting to burst into flame—but she will never leave it, and who would have the heart to make her? Who *could* make her? Who knows what's under those piles of papers and board games? Who wants to know? But the organization of all of it is simple: here for awhile, then shipped tomorrow to someone who needs it. In this way her house is a perpetually revolving carnival of forlorn objects, a halfway house for dolls and dresses in transit.

At Christmas she sends my parents a huge, beat-up box. If we are lucky enough to all be together, we gather round the great box in the living room and crack nervous jokes about its contents. It is a profound ritual of the absurd, a little unnerving for the uninitiated. For there is no correlation whatever between fashion or perceived need in her gifts; there is no way to predict or even anticipate what's in the gigantic, bulging box. It could contain a shower curtain with Daffy Duck or rock-'n'-roll china, a velvet suitcase or a pewter flute, a crystal serving ladle or oven mitts. Whatever is in there is in there only because it is a kind of fate: whatever is in there comes from an irrevocable time and place, rocking out of nowhere, crazy because that is the only word we have for it. In thirty years of seeing the Great Mystery Box arrive and waiting to open it, there has never once been a correct or even approximate guess or prognostication. All bets are off. It sits near the tree like a bomb of laughing gas waiting to go off. We laugh because there is nothing else to do. We laugh because we do not know her, because deep within all of us this kind of chaos reigns, too, and the force of this chaos sends laughter through our throats, life-laughter, the laughter of the life force she continues to give us like a burst of cold air every Christmas. We laugh because no one else is quite this alive, this unpredictable in the face of marching time. We laugh because we need this disorder desperately and she provides it each year—the trickster throwing a monkey wrench into all our preconceptions; we laugh because she laughs *with* life, the laughter of cedar branches, the laughter of water over rocks, the laughter that is her living legacy in the face of all we will become.

So one Christmas there was an Elvis soap-on-a-rope, monographed handkerchiefs (no one's initials), a calendar of painted farm horses, matching pink ear muffs, and a glass coin holder that separated change into funky rainbow columns. At the bottom of it was a wind-up turnkey that played the theme from *The Sound of Music*. We laughed very hard. Because what better gift is there than a side-splitting, unexpected guffaw that has no destination or purpose beyond itself? How often does unexpected laughter come into our lives? How many more times can we count on it coming out of thin air, giving us in that very moment everything we will ever need?

Between the river course of dying and writing letters to all her children and their children and their children, she expands the parameters of other lives. She sends letters, checks all over the country; she sends a piece of herself each time in scrawled handwriting that recounts her bowling scores or anecdotes from the flea market. I have never once received a letter from her that did not contain money. One day my dad ventured into the house with her, and they went downstairs. Among the legions of toys and boxes and belts, she produced a coffee can with over $5,000 in cash. She uncorked this surprise for my father and gave him the whole thing—he who was a successful businessman. She has been living solely on Social Security now for twenty years—well under the official poverty level. I try to picture him holding the Folgers can stuffed with cash, groping for words. He didn't need or want it and neither, apparently, did she. It was the gesture that mattered, and everything leading up to it; it was that she was here giving away her life fortune in a coffee can so easily, with no doubt or equivocation. Here, it's all yours, she said; I don't need it. What, then, does she need? And how can I learn to need that, too? Money has never been important to her beyond a certain amount; money and banks . . . She never showed up on their computer screens anyway. My grandfather and she never invested in any stock market or mutual fund—or for that matter, in any banks. The Depression scarred them not in fear but in something far nobler: they would get by because they had each other and they knew how to survive. What dwindled could be shored up with hard work. No one lives forever anyway. They worked all their lives because there was no other choice—and at the end of work, they gave what they had away. Then on to the next flea market, the next round of business; the squirrels still need to be fed. Now she finally has a joint checking account presided over by my aunt. But she and my grandfather have always been wary of large institutions.

I think I know what "salt of the earth" means. I know that salt is bitter and prodigal, that it flavors all food, that one can choke on it and die of thirst from it in the sea. I know that salt is real and broken down from licks on the shores. I know that animals come from all over to lick at rocks to restore their bodies. Salt is what we are after when all the frills and nonsense are stripped or grinded away; salt is a good thing if that is all you're born with, because it is all you will die with. Salt blows in the wind and stings the eye. Salt is the communion of food and the body, the back pocket of the taste buds where all necessity springs. Salt is the first silt of our dreams, and we need it for the long haul across any kind of landscape. We need salt because after all the gaudy and false flavors, salt is the bedrock of earth. It is the sperm and egg of life, and it flows through our veins like salt water deep down in the salt-worn cornices of sea caves. Salt is the earth and the sea. I come from salt people. Salt of the earth, the people of salt who withstand all weather and travail and feed us in the bitter crystals of life, living and dying their hard-working lives so that others can get by, at least for a little while.

Back to the house again, where you are safe only if you talk to the dolls, the congress of childhood and adults who need them, the long bridge between dreaming and waking. She is patiently talking to each one of them, telling them about this or that, to not be afraid, the trip in the mail will be worth it. With them she is herself. In one of the dolls' heads a mouse is building a nest, and the cracked head gives a brief peephole to life. Nestled in a bowl at the back of the head, the mouse sleeps and waits into morning. Doll's eyes bright button blue and infinite, keep staring in the way of all glass. This tenant will not be usurped — not in this warehouse of a house. Not now or ever.

I pity those who consider eccentricity an embarrassment or a symptom; rather, it is something earned if it is genuine, a long response to the unfairness of this life. My grandmother has this — indeed it is through her that I learned of it, how to recognize the real thing and to celebrate it. I know in this age of glamour and fools the real things are often hidden; they reside in dwellings invisible to most. I know history has become at best a byword or a tag to put on something transient and false, Super Bowls or game shows. But here is a woman who has no room for that: all of the nonsensical and ephemeral has been pushed out of her life by necessity so that only something genuine and solid remains. Here it is: a house of dolls. Come on in and be a child again.

Who knows what she could have been in a different day and age, under different circumstances, with her punky wit and original way of regarding the world? She is a figure of staggering hope and influence; the whole family revolves around her like colors on a pinwheel. Such simple peace after a life of hard work, near-poverty, illness, mortgages, a son in jail, ache upon chronic ache, work, work, work, and more work, distrust of doctors and dentists, phrases of Hungarian in her dreams, life savings kept in a coffee can in the trunk of a car, staple guns, sickly, sweet-smelling effluvium of the paper mill, cankers, long early mornings, kolaches, hot stalls at the flea market buzzing with flies, card games, cheap wine, on and on into the catalogue of holding on with humor, toughness, and grace. What I do not understand is how someone can appear both so ridiculous and so dignified all at once. Nothing impresses her, not money, not clothes, not learning. I have never met a woman so sure of herself who yet takes herself so lightly; maybe this is a mechanism of survival that has become a virtue all its own. When she is in a room everyone else seems drab and a little wooden: she is like a slow-burning firecracker. Once she was playing a serious game of cards and for no reason at all she placed a pair of chattering teeth on the table. Everyone busted up, she busted up, but no one knew what it meant.

On hot summer nights she sleeps alone in her over-stuffed house, and the lack of ventilation or air conditioning must be stifling. All her buys have nearly succeeded in blotting out her windows completely. Stacks and rows of stuff five-feet tall cut off midriff views; and the odd thing is they just teeter there, growing inch by inch each year until her house is not a house at all but a chaotic back room of a Salvation Army. My dad shudders to go there. He is so neat and clean; how can he confront his own mother, who keeps bringing home loads in shopping bags? From the outside the house looks condemned, each window a strata of debris. If you wait long enough and ask her, anything in the world you need can be found in the staggering piles. You need bookends, Rose Bowl napkins, picture frames? Do you need coffee pots or teacups, a monkey with cymbals? Are you looking for a wicker chair or a Swiss Army knife? How about a grandfather clock with a ball-capped cuckoo? Flapper attire, cigarette holders? Lava lamps and Johnny Carson memorabilia? How about the '52 Tigers or an autographed picture of Sparky Anderson? It's all here, waiting for you to take it away.

It is no longer up to me to pass judgment on these things. Only that I hope I learn to read in the same way that my grandmother collects dolls, that I'll know a bargain when I see one. I need not fear an avalanche in my heart. The rays of the sun and moon will touch me. And now her light is growing more distant each day, getting fainter where before I thought it would shine forever. I hope she found the right stone. I can see the stone held in the light of the woman in the water, the clear, white light that for a moment became a reason and an essence I did not fear anything until she stepped into the shadows.

The Dignity of Crumbs

MY NEIGHBOR IS SO OLD that she cracked a vertebra while bending to pick up a letter. Shuffling toward the kitchen, she was on her way to the dining room table when the letter slipped from her hand. She bent to pick it up. But too quickly: I imagine the sound of her back was like the click of a gear lock, or a key turning in a rusty door. It was a mechanical sound, and it scared her very much. It was not pain she felt but surprise and embarrassment, like a part of her own body was playing a cruel joke on her: "See: this is the price you pay for daring to be independent at an old age." She managed to crab her way to a chair where she sat crosswise, feet up, to keep the rest of her back from breaking.

I picture her after the break, her heart beating faster, as she moved in slow, painful contortions to the chair, frightened about what to do next. What can you do when the body breaks down, one precious rib or hipbone at a time? She must have cried out, but of course no one was there. No one is ever there at such crucial moments. No one is there to hear the delicate crack of the ninety-four-year-old woman, to watch the shuffling motion, to placate. She was all alone in her sun-veiled rooms. This is the hard part with the old: few people are there to see them breaking down, to watch the dry shell of the body crack open one seam at a time. It happens mostly in shuttered privacy, where each small accident hints at the body's own downhill progression, the dissolution of days and nights. Always, always, always the body. They suffer the indignity of their failing bodies one small click or boil at a time, a vision of hell that goes unappreciated, I suspect, until we live it ourselves with our own decalcifying bones.

Part of the dread of living next to Katherine is wondering how she will be found one day—and who will do the finding. This worry is not macabre but based on the conditions of her dwindling life—and mine. Not I, I think—though this is hopelessly selfish. I don't want to find her passed out or worse, because I don't want the burden, but somehow she keeps dragging me back into the land of human responsibility, asking me without words to be there, Please be there to help me. Helping her (it is too grand a phrase) is a special burden, a reckoning with fate, for when the body closes shop someone must be there to turn off the lights, to lock the doors and clean up the little, incontinent puddles, to sweep away the last of the woodchips, and to weep at the dusty window.

Katherine's furniture is arranged at key points in her apartment so that she can navigate by touch the treacherous wooden floors of our building, the hard angles of unforgiving doors. All of it is a trial to be gotten through, to be loved, feared, and loathed for its own sake, something to pray for—and against.

Once smoke billowed out of her apartment, and I banged on her latticed outer door. Smoke seeped out between the slits, like an eerie, infernal hell-mouth. She shuffled to greet me and in a shaken voice told me her toaster had overheated—would I mind opening a window to let the smoke out? I entered into a haze of smoke and opened the window. She stood behind me trembling: I felt awkward, valiant, and embarrassed all at once. Could you buy me some bread? she asked timidly; she would gladly pay me back, only now the last of her bread was burnt to a crisp. See: and she held up the black, bitter mitts, darker than tar.

Part of me wanted to tell her that she should no longer make toast; that she must do without it; that she could not risk her luck with electric coils and glowing heat. I wanted to say (though now it sounds monstrous), You're too old to have toast, you can't put yourself in danger. I was in the position of telling her what her friends had been saying for years: you're too old to live on your own; it's time to give up your home and move to a place where others can take care of you. I hovered on the verge of a kind of judgment, a decision laid at the feet of a near disaster. Smoke? Did you say smoke? You have forfeited the right of your toaster: then your microwave, your oven, your knives, your bathtub, down and down the chain of devices which symbolize independence, the ability to cook and clean for yourself. All of it is gone: you are no longer fit to live here, you can forget about that now. The rest of us can't keep bailing you out.

Who is she to me after all? An erstwhile stranger, a neighbor I hear using her sink on the other side of mine, a quiet, mouse-like (though determined) woman? I am not bound to her by blood or choice, only the proximity of rented rooms. I never asked for this, I never asked to be drawn into your aging woman's life, a stranger, a neighbor. I did not ask to get involved. All I wanted was to be left alone, to exchange a few courtesies in the hallway. Can't you see I'm struggling for my own life here, my own place in the world? In her kitchen that day I was in the sudden position of executioner, the one sympathetic soul that could turn hostile by passing my own dark judgment. The old are inconvenient: they call at strange hours, they ask us to take out their trash, to close their windows, to investigate odd noises. They draw us into their fears, the tremolo of their hearts. They ask us first and always to understand small bruises, hidden hurts, the spanning yawn of loneliness. They ask us to be patiently human at all times. I stood poised in her kitchen between sympathy and dismissal. I was a monster of flickering half-light, buffeted by unreasonable irritation and understanding.

Then I saw her toaster, an old, reliable Quasar, and the irritation just fell away. I suddenly felt ashamed, horrified that I could leap to such ready-made conclusions. Surely, this could happen to anyone; surely her need for toast was reasonable, specific, beautiful in a way: it was a part of the day's routine, a simple blessing. We studied the toaster together. We turned it over and shook it free of crumbs, which came out in a sprinkle of gold, like glitter. We turned it on. We waited in silence for the coils to glow, the small hum to sound, the heat to rise in the two wide slits. We waited in hope. The toaster worked fine. Katherine's hands were steady and firm. She told me how she was talking to her brother on the phone when the smoke rose, of her quick good-bye. All of it was handled perfectly. She wasn't strong enough to get the window up. That was all. She asked me to buy a loaf of bread—that basic staple of all human nourishment—and I was struck by the simplicity of the request, the sanctity of it. Bread to have in the morning. Bread for toast. Crumbs. At one hundred pounds she needed bread and fat, she needed so much. It was like she was asking for time, for another day or week in her own apartment, among her own cherished things and memories. I bought her the bread, a simple transaction. I left it outside her door. I saw that she took it. I imagined a spotted, beautiful hand dropping a slice into the toaster. I pictured her waiting, welcoming the heat, arms crossed in her blue cardigan, hunched against the draft. These things are realities, the high-ceilinged kitchen, the tiny woman, the glowing hum of the toaster that works the bread into a scorched plain, an infinite, minuscule, delectable feast. Her life is fading, slowing down, the memories come on, gather like shadows in the flickering light—and the toast pops up in the electric silence.

Now I think the world is full of tiny, invisible strings we're scarcely aware of, of threaded gossamer so delicate it binds us to people and to places and the nethermost of gestures, to the tiny warblings of living beings, to the musty smells of other rooms. The strings tying us to each other are everywhere. We are connected to others in a spanning web: it is our job not to tear it, to keep it in good repair, even if we cannot see it.

I can no longer call myself a stranger to Katherine. I have given up that right long ago. I have washed her underwear, closed her windows, brought her mail, fetched her prescriptions. I have sat in her living room while she told me stories of her farmer father, his talent for making boots, his long clay pipe. I have sat impatient and restless, brick red rising on my neck to get out, out, out—Can't you see I need to go?—as time was held in abeyance and the eerie light of memory shone through her eyes. She has lived her whole life raising other people's children. She never married. She likes to collect stuffed frogs. The light tumbles into our apartments at the same time, we rise in the dark together. I hear her in the morning on the other side of the wall as she must hear me; both of us make coffee in the early morning. We live in different times, different places. I don't have rogue whiskers sprouting from my chin; she doesn't need to ice her ankle after basketball. The threads spool out from the invisible orb, spinning, spinning. On some days age is an arbitrary number: the mind is clear, memories collide in fresh colors, we know joy is timeless and brief. All ages disintegrate beyond matter into a single, unaccountable filament. We laugh and joke, remember, pull each other's leg: this joy is not subject to the parameters of age.

Her renegade wit still catches me off-guard, she still puts me in my whipper-snapper place by turning an odd phrase into a gentle reminder, by saying, "Bob, I don't know where the time goes, but you shouldn't think it goes by itself." I look around her room, fiddle with my hands, grow a little confused. Did I miss something? What is she talking about? I see a gleam in her eyes, something a little too sharp, too crafty: and then I know she knows I am doing this for largely the wrong reasons, for my own selfish, secret self, that I don't really understand anything, that she is watching me and following my actions—that in sometimes helping her she forgives me for my own true thoughts, which are not always pure and good, but grudging, petty, full of constraints. Sometimes she sees I am not helping her for her own sake, but to let myself off the hook—that she still has much to teach me about human responsibility and the deep bass notes of real compassion.

Crumbs multiply, scatter, are swept into the sink. She nibbles on a piece of toast. Her hands are porcelain curves with blue veins that work a little harder each day to reach all of the extremities. Old age, old age, old age, the mantra is everywhere. To get from one room to another requires patience and effort, so much: she is like a spider walking across a blank wall, pushing her walker before her. Into the living room, into the hallway. Her apartment is cleaned by Merry Maids once a month. She knows where everything is. Every week someone calls to scare her into moving: she is not going, now or ever. If that means someone must come in and do her wash; if that means a nurse must check on her every two days; if that means she must have groceries delivered, or that someone—anyone—must someday find her passed out on the floor, then so be it. She will rely on the kindness of others, in fact she will demand it in her own gentle, unyielding way. She brings out the helpfulness in everyone, the pity and the spite. She is dug in for the final, long haul. And when she drops off to sleep in her armchair at twilight, she hears all the familiar sounds, the knocking of old heaters, the banging of doors, the wind through the giant trees. She closes her eyes and dozes, not quite asleep in the material moment, rearranging her needs and desires, shuffling them between her old woman wants and the play of memory.

Signs

The Dark Hangnails of God

LAST WINTER I was followed by crows. They waited for me in
barren trees that waved crazily in the cold January wind; they
waited for me outside on a supermarket roof, lined up like a death
squad, heavy-hooded, bare-chested, staring vacantly from their ancient glass eyes; they followed me on walks, hopping in the middle of
the street like madmen come down to mock me; I saw one of them
pick at a Burger King wrapper on the sidewalk and shimmy down a
cold fry like a shot of rye whiskey. One even stood vigil outside the
neighborhood library, three stories up in a naked elm: she was beautiful against the white sky (I call it "she" on a hunch, out of hope),
holding on to one slender twig that defied my sense of balance and
proportion. How could she stand there at the top of everything, hanging on to a thread of tree? But there she was, perfectly poised, her roof
the sky as her black feathers were lifted but not ruffled by the buffeting
wind. The branch went up and down, loop-the-loop, each revolution
a small, haunting reminder that she'd been here before. I stood there
many minutes staring at her perfect aloneness. She was moved neither
by loud noise nor by any other distraction: she was seeing the wind,
tasting it through her scimitar beak. It was clean and pure and went
through her wings, like a light sweeping down a dark hallway. Some
call them scavengers, but the only phrase that came to my mind was
the dark hangnails of God.

For two months last winter they were everywhere—and the snow
took on new meaning each time it fell, crow fodder and crow meaning
where everything was white, blank, beautiful, and merciless.

One night I dreamt they were out there, circling the apartment in great
numbers, staring through the walls and windows to the middle of my

bones: they wanted to have me, eviscerated but alive, out there in the white open where everything was plain to see. They were flying around in circles high above the trees, their black wings so many planks of death waiting in the blanked-out sky, eyes the size of Christmas bulbs hung from a tree and staring back in odorous greens. Their world was not my world, except for where I would end up, indeed where we all end up: at the mercy of scavengers or time or the fatal combination of both. Crows do not so much announce these facts as embody them, in each swoop and turn of their bodies or in the gangly plunder of their walking. In my dream they were nearer than fear, close up; they seemed to come out of the purpose of my life like dead relatives or the common chant of a tribe I couldn't name.

One crow was apart from the rest, miles away in a tree. On that high perch she was riding the roller coaster of life and death, and watched me patiently from afar. It was her patience and beauty that moved me to recognize that we were both in this dream together, caught at the wrist and the wing, and together we would sooner or later succumb to the inescapable dichotomy of living and dying. I did not die in the dream but saw it coming like a cold wing turned sideways and blown directly to my hand where I could touch and feel its black heaviness that became lightness after a while—it turned white while I watched, peeling back its true color until the blackness was a memory that faded like dusk or evening. The new wing, the one that I came to hold, evolved out of the old as necessarily as the turning of leaves, or watching a kind man's hair go through a lifetime of loss, travail, and ineffable small joys in a few brief seconds: it was a shock to come this far in the weird timelessness of a dream, as I knew the crows were still circling, and the she-crow was watching from her distant perch that made her the queen of crows, or the one who had flown away to be my guardian and killer on the edge of a dream.

All of this happened instantly, yet took a night to unfold. There was no sound to this dream, just silence and waiting. I expect no one to believe me: but her wing, her dark presence got me moving in a new direction, past the banality of my own life into the greater migration we cannot name. She came to warn me. It was all right to be afraid but somehow beside the point. The point was her perch and vigil miles

82

from here in a dream, where even now I can see the tremendous thrashing of the trees and her simple hold on a top branch so beautiful and calm I can only call it finality in the terrible grace of a life coming to its end.

Crows remind us that we come from the natural world and will return to it one day, whether we want to or not. They are emissaries of that world and keep vigil over everything because it is their purpose to do so. But in this dream they were waiting, and I cannot say I was fully afraid, for in their blue-black wings there was something necessary for me to recognize and to understand, some glimpse of another world and reckoning that I had up until now ignored or forgotten but knew a long, long time ago. High above they were waiting for me to come out and join them; they would not attack; they were simply awaiting the natural, inevitable catastrophe that would lure me out, and then they would do their proper job of wiping my body clean from the face of the earth.

It was one of those winter nights that swells in secrecy, each drift and swirl of snow another movement toward some uncompleted monument. But there were no crows. I watched the snow whip up a snowstorm before my window and tumble under the gray street lights that stared unblinking like a night watchman on his last cup of coffee. I went back to bed and remembered the green glass eyes that showed myself looking back, even as they floated and careened over the sleeping world. The wind rattled the apartment, as one more night slipped away to darkness and winter.

II

Every late afternoon crows came from all over to stand and *caw* in a neighbor's trees. I could not figure it out. After I realized the crows were watching me (or so I almost believed), I started to watch for them. I trudged the narrow shoveled ravines of sidewalks and followed them to a single tree that held them like a scattering of pepper. Some perched apart from the rest in nearby trees. I stood under a stark oak looking up. Then such a stillness came over me, a recognition of something greater, the natural world come down to visit in a midtown neighborhood where the houses are close together and mantled with snow, crows to bring the winter sky into sharper focus. It was not that they were here together, waiting something out; it was that they'd been here all along. Everything around them was an approximation of their intent, as I watched them heel-bound on earth. They were high up and grimmer than cold. They were built for their purpose. They wore the naked camouflage of death.

I looked for them every afternoon and lost myself in the process; just these black birds holding to a ritual older than human kind, which for my meager understanding I had come to watch. If they were really symbols of foreboding and decline, why not go all the way? I had crows on the brain, heard their calls everywhere. They would not leave me alone. Sometimes an animal and a person can collide and become a fugue, a time and two movements together that for however briefly mark them as partners in a dance the person comes to recognize as significant to him or to her: the animal, of course, is usually oblivious. I don't know what they wanted. I don't know what I wanted, gawking at them from the ground every late afternoon. But even here on the sidewalk I was a part of something, the spectacle of winter and sacrifice, as lights in the houses began to glow and the world turned darker.

I imagined they were talking to set the world straight, that the cacophony of their caws matched the direness of cold and ice. They were talking in response to the season, something we have lost the ability to do. Their talk was the screech of stone on stone, wave becoming foam, the almost human plea of loneliness in the universe; for each crow, I noticed, was talking to herself, looking away, not holding dialogue with anyone but the immutable and silent all that binds everything together, you and me, crow and wrapper, weather vane and snowman. From the harsh beseeching of their cries you could tell they did not expect response, but crying out seemed to make the burden (whatever it was) less great, less a prayer than a need to make noise for its own sake, for their own sake, to see and make sure that the equipment of living was still valid. They were checking their parts, going over them piece by piece, confirming their efficiently knit wings as the clouds moved on mile by epic mile above them. I watched them every afternoon until my wife asked me, "Where are you going?" and I answered in all complicity, "I'm going to follow the crows."

One day the racket became too much and a man came out on his porch with a shotgun and fired a round into the sky. The crows scattered. They took off into such an elegant and purposeful flight that I did not think it only fear, although surely that had been the cause; they took off in all directions, blowing apart, and I thought then maybe they knew something we didn't: that they'd be back, not to sneer or taunt, but because it was their rightful place to pick up where they left off, regardless of interference. They were brainless motes in the sky, coming apart in all directions, I do not know how they kept themselves up until distance vanished them speck by speck, wing by wing.

III

You've been waiting for a story to see how these things connect: you've been waiting for a reason why crows visited me one winter and why I paid them mind. I do not have an answer. I simply turned around and they were there. I began to notice them everywhere: in parks, trees, and benches; on roofs, sidewalks, and parked cars; in a ramshackle alleyway between spilled garbage cans of debris and frayed tires. We bumped into each other and stared each other down. Sometimes they came upon me unawares, like the subconscious relics of old dreams and fears. One crow looked at me with a belt in its beak, tarnished buckle on the end hanging like the lolling head of a doll that had been snatched from the Tuesday pickup, discarded here because childhood was finally over. You can believe that of people and crows: that they work in symbiosis, that crows pick up what we leave off, that they have the final say by picking us up when we pass over the killing mound of time and decrepitude. How could it be different? If "all ages are equidistant from God" as Leopold von Ranke once said, then crows know this and do their jobs of erasure and maintenance, no other, combing the ground with their huge eyes whether we ride a horse or drive a Ford.

Sometimes winter has this effect of emphasizing the profound negatives, the things we cannot escape or the things we try to avoid. Being people, we want comfort and consolation. In winter (and crows) there is none. Just a sweeping aside of buds and flowers until the branches are bare, as we huddle inside in wool socks or take baths while the TV blares with a freakish light and the black birds circle and wait, circle and wait. Once I began to look for them I saw that they came out of the fabric of the past and present, were agents of history themselves, veering into the future, as they knew something I didn't. I knew they were only animals, but somehow their presence became something else, a reckoning or harbinger of something I could not name. So I looked for them singly and en masse; I began to chart their progress and work out a system of hypothesis whereby I could predict and understand their powwows in the sky and sudden defection by twos or threes to other high places. It never came together. For the paradox of crows is that they wait high up and then get in close where the work is dirty, offal and aftermath, manipulating with their own mouths and tongues that which we would touch only with sticks and rubber gloves; they are not glamorous birds, but in that they clean up the waste of those who came before. They are time janitors, and their glory comes from action, not knowledge. They know the final score before the players have even arrived. This is why we respect and hate them: because they dwell in death as we ourselves dwell in death but with a simpler force and recognition. If you look for crows you will find them, and not only in the archetypal places. They will find you anywhere. And really I was no different: they watched and saw everything. I was just a part of the moving landscape that briefly caught their eye.

I dusted off an old *Encyclopædia Britannica* and looked for some kind of explanation, circa 1958:

Crow, a general name for several birds of the genus Corvus *of the family* Corvidae. *It is applied particularly in England to the carrion crow (C. corone) and hooded crow (C. cornix) and in America to the American crow (C. brachyrhynchos). The* Corvidae *are the most highly developed family of birds, and include, besides the crows proper, the magpies, jays, choughs, the rook and the raven.*

Not much here. The entry went on to portray and explain the crow in very general terms, in terms of its scavenging and migration habits. It was up to me to make personal sense of the bird. They would not stay still in the pages of the encyclopedia; would not, in fact, reveal themselves except as outlines of a shadow creeping forward in awful sloping inertia.

How we become bird watchers is always a mystical event, something between waiting for God and watching for Him in winged particulars. Birds are moving souls. The magic of the sparrow or the robin is their ordinary exercise of magic in a world where magic is often hidden; they prefer to be spectacular just by being themselves, perching on a wire and then diving off in arcs toward the ground. They don't need our linguistic hang-ups, our need to make money or take vacations. They have the whole world in their wings.

But the crow is different: it won't sacrifice purpose to dazzlement, vigilance for beautiful singing. The crow is not a performer but a grim participant; I sometimes think that is why they are hounded in the sky by other birds: because they are not theatrical or brightly plumed or possessive of any trait that makes you want to keep one for a pet. They are built perfectly for the work at hand, and the work at hand is always up close and terrible. They do not have the majesty of hawks or eagles. They are somehow outside of time. And that is why they hold such menace and mystery.

IV

During that same time I started a poem. The poem is still unfinished, but the second stanza is pertinent here, something that for a time gave me no peace.

> *Only the crows watch now,*
> *recording the movement of footfall on ice*
> *as old women throw breadcrumbs to the sparrows*
> *or scatter a few kernels of corn from the back door.*
> *Do they wait to see what will happen?*
> *Do they wait to see what we will we do?*
> *But they know what we will do.*
> *We will do nothing.*

If you take a bird and focus on it, you run the risk of making it your prophet. Many people seem to work just this way: by the power of suggestion and the power of symbol to become manifest in their lives. For some it is the $ sign, green cut grass in the suburbs, a new pair of running shoes. I am susceptible to all these, but arching above them is the presence of the natural world, even where nature is cramped and crowded out (seemingly) by jets overhead and rush hour traffic. We can't seem to avoid it forever, which is why those crows have the final say. I had no business following them or trying to figure out their methods, except that I am a living creature myself. So putting on my boots at the end of the day and walking out into winter stillness seemed to be a necessary corridor I had to enter. When you get right down to it, none of us is spared, so why not follow the instruments of transfer for a few days when you don't think they're looking?

When you find a crow close up, take a careful look and see what's in its eyes: if the angle of light is right you are likely to see yourself diminished and staring back, just a window of pale light that seems minuscule in the daytime but for its absence the whole world would roll over in darkness, betray you in leaving. You are not looking for yourself in those eyes but the glimmer of a hope that gleams there like a hand-held star. No matter how large the wings or gaping the mouth, the star is what there is to save the crow and you from final damnation; and the crow becomes the hideous bird that carries brightness in its beak, or the radiance of a sun you must squint at to notice. Then there is a reason for all that loathing and dread, and the reason is itself a sacrifice to knowing deeper than mere understanding. Because the body knows what the mind refuses to acknowledge: a certain creeping forward over the cattails of a life, over thorns and berry bushes. Seeing it is the one grace we have. Crows help us to see it. They confront with their blackness the terror in ourselves. Common bird, crow is the sacrament of death and is therefore valid in a park or on a windowpane—and it will not give up its place as the worker of a mystery.

I imagine another dream like the crow, but in this one she is resting on my arm, wings spread and beak apart, as I feed her a cracker or bit of bread. She gawks at me in surprise, tearing the food from my hand but not splitting the skin. On a wire two feet long she is tied to my arm, I carry and balance her like a statue and move around in slow circles to show her off in all light. She pirouettes with me, eye to eye, wings outstretched for balance while my free arm does the same. We're in a dance of life and death, turning slowly on the axis of our bodies.

We lock souls as we are tied together, myself a little cringed that at any moment she will go for my eyes and I will dash her down against a stone. As long as we're moving everything is all right, as movement becomes the antidote to sudden violence. Like all living parts, we must hang together or forgo movement. But the violence is always there, waiting, not hidden away, just separated by a stare and a turn. I hate and love this bird equally, just as I hate and love my own small life that is scraping and soaring by turns. We both know how the dream will end, but for now the movement calms us, as the dance continues. And it will continue, for seconds, hours, or years; and I must not flinch or look away, because looking away would be sacrilege in the crow's eyes, as it would be in mine. The snow is thick, the sky is gray, and the wood is stacked for the fireplace. But first I must gaze in to the crow's eyes, as she must gaze into mine.

The Tides, the Tides

I

N A FEW HOURS the sun will go down. People I do not know, people I will never meet, walk by, intent on their own internal weather. It has always been thus: pot bellies, loose shirts, stubble, cigars, handbags, a woman carrying a leash unattached to any dog, creased faces, chained wallets, a life, a life.

When they go by, I stare at them until they are past and wonder what all of it could mean. These are the mysteries, the flip-flops of the homeless woman in hundred-degree weather, toting her life behind her in dusty black bags as she stares off into something clear or foggy, the narrow portholes of destiny. This is not New York or Chicago or Miami. Just Omaha, the "O" starting out in eternity, "Maha" ending in a feeble trebled note, the wobbling of bad axles or broken faith, the ingrained sorrow of tiny failures. Here you see clouds unobstructed by almost any building—or put in high relief, clouds, sky, and glass forming their own kind of pirouette that will never come this way again. They drift by in designs of mythic grandeur, the only thing this hilly downtown reveals of fleeting greatness. I have been here all of my life, staring out such windows. Who am I to question what it means? Cannot I not love it here as well as somewhere else? I don't know if Omaha (that lovely, heart-breaking word) is a good place or a bad place, an upstart or a lagger. I don't know if people come here to start over or to give up, to raise kids or save money. I don't know. I have been here all of my life.

When I worked a temporary job downtown, transcribing insurance claims, I wore headphones all day, listening to witnesses of traffic accidents from all over the country. I heard their accents, the rounding and hip-hop of local dialects from Houston, Boston, Boca Raton. What they saw and didn't see: the unstrapped driver who slammed his rusting van into a telephone pole; the group of kids in the tinted Malibu who ran a stop sign and clipped a Chevy. I heard these claims and typed them in all day long, the atonal music of the bureaucratic machine, voices without faces, the pauses, ellipses, rainy weather, slick roads, planetary seams of cracked windshields. And the whole time I would cast my glance once, twice, three times out the window in the space of a minute, the outside of downtown Omaha, where the buildings (it is true) are set upon steeply sloping hills, tilting under the same sky that devours the Gobi and the Sahara. This was the essential, mystical Omaha to me, learning to worship the sky. You had no real choice in the matter, the sky was all you had each day, the tides coming in, the tides going out, and you smack in the middle of it, helpless before zenith and sundown.

In summer, if you stared out these windows long enough, even as you listened to the voices of people trying to get their facts straight, you developed a pattern, a need, a lifting-up of your own spirit that had nothing to do with faith or fine feelings; you could drift partway into the atmosphere, rise up out of your seat, become a dust mote or a lilting scrap of paper that was shooting for the clouds in slipping spoons of pendulum rising, accompanied by voices. You had no choice if your spirit was intact. And with the calm questions of the trained investigator (questions never veering from the hide-bound script), you could, once in a while, be lifted out of yourself into contemplation of this same searing sky, the sky of Bowles, the sky of Arab shepherds, lost cowboys. I would listen to the voices, learn to memorize their cadence, take them home with me at night— "He, I donno, he said he was going to the corner for a soda and some grits" —watch this sky unfold in infinite blue, swirls of dust coming from the construction site that was the beginning of a skyscraper. Skyscraper: you became that word, scraping the sky from a chair, the only gift an insurance firm would ever give you. I became a part of the sky gradually, I couldn't avoid it; by two o'clock in the hot afternoon I was drifting, drifting upward like an unmoored balloon.

This is Omaha to me, sky blazing, courting contemplation or drop-dead boredom in an insurance office, where your cubicle is like everyone else's, save for the personal effects of photographs, stuffed animals, or inspirational calendars. I chose not to decorate my temporary desk—it was stripped clean, bare as a bone, only the key essentials vying for any space. I came from nowhere and would return to nowhere without a scrap of evidence to show that I was here.

There had to be another way for all these people, ladies who read romance novels on break, my neighbor who confided in me that he smokes pot every day. I smelled a dim kind of desperation in there, tangled paperclips in the carpet, coffee stains, ergonomic plastic, that officey smell that is always one nuance away from the fragrance of hell. But those voices, that noontime sky, the tides of hysteria laid down by routine, the soft, diminishing clicks of several keyboards going at once. Sometimes just sitting there it was like my own life had never been; I had never run with my shirt off, watched grasshoppers, eaten ice cream. The pall of the office was like official penance sanctioned by the moon, a lunar setting of unreality. I was plugged into one aspect of the essential Omaha, its invisible dynamo that moves all other shakers: insurance for insurance's sake. Appalling, ubiquitous insurance, insurance that covered everything under the sun: cars, ovens, disabled veterans, renters, home, fire, theft, life, prosthesis, hair, wig, registered weapon. Jewelry, computers, a precocious singing voice, old photographs of movie stars. I knew then (rather slowly, a realization I had not considered before) that insurance could add up to a whole world-view; that in its most radical and rational form it could replace religion, faith, the birth of small babies; that Omaha, my beloved and loathed hometown for all these years, paid homage mostly to this vast, intricate way of life, that houses in west Omaha with well-trimmed lawns and winding stone paths to the mailbox were the direct and indirect result of my own transcriptions, my bearing of witness to these other witnesses, all of our voices going down into well-regulated paths of decorum and irrefutable proof, that what we needed, by God, was an airtight case to claim our settlement, our cash, our new lawn chairs. Little if any of it had to do with goodness or wisdom. It was all business, covering each other's backs, sawing the legs off false claims so that they would never walk again. In my way I was a small executioner of a bigger pattern, a clean-cut soldier on the battlefield of defense and prosecution. So many tapes, so much bent and broken metal, crossed lines, questionable breath: the whole country seemed, then, to throb with a deeper, bureaucratic insistence, as if TV and movies had thwarted the nation from the real business at hand. Omaha is a key hub around which these pinwheels fly, thin spokes of information that add up to an industry, an economy, a nation, a huge and spectacular wheel. I was floored, unsettled. Someone had socked me in the gut, sabotaged my dreams. I took my fifteen minute breaks as if I were stealing my own sanity back from the sky, clouds I knew had no truck with the auto industry and its great overseer, insurance.

I could breathe outside again, become human again. I looked at the homeless people with new awareness and respect; I sat on a park bench and studied the soft interior glow of spilled popcorn on the sidewalk. Could people really spend their whole working lives inside such offices? Could they really be that heroic and that far gone? Could they really listen all day every day to José in San Antonio, Lisa in Brooklyn, Jo-Jo in Dallas? I imagined the people behind these voices, their cotton shifts and underwear, their cheap and expensive jewelry, small dogs barking in the background. From Lenny in New York I even heard traffic in the background, car horns, the rasping of traffic. Lenny from New York, patient, funny Lenny who gave his account with good humor and local color, who clearly enjoyed talking for talking's sake (and knew that he was in the clear); my one-way friend Lenny who liked to talk, veered off obliquely into comments about his teeth, the cat who wouldn't get down from the kitchen table, the humidity and heat of midsummer in Manhattan. But Lenny was one in a million. Most people were not this generous, this amused at the routine unfolding before them. If they only knew how many others had suffered this same script, how many others were also right and also wrong, how many expected in some dim, heartbreaking way that this settlement would change their lives forever. I took my break, read a few pages from the book I carried with me, and went back inside to lose myself in voices and the sky.

Some days I thought I could do this work for awhile, maybe for a long, long time; no one bothered me, people were very nice, I could henpeck my through the day and even my life if I wanted to in a cool, air-conditioned room with unlimited access to the sky. I could love my mother and father all over again, imagine their childhoods, their Patsy Cline. I could become all brain and fiber, look purely into the sky, lose myself, daydream into the ether of the atmosphere. But I could also imagine going slowly mad, woefully depressed for no clear-cut reason: I could imagine stalking a mouse with an exposed stapler, wear blood on my shirt, a feather behind my ear. The word *temporary* saved me. I was *temporary*. The job was *temporary*. But the claims I transcribed were permanent, mounted in a warehouse or file of mammoth proportions, so many voices on tape, so many fingers that did the typing. Where did they go, and who kept count? How often again were these voices listened to, if ever? What do you do with these recorded voices, strangers who woke up in their creaky beds, rubbing their eyes, this day like all days just a little closer to death? All of us lived in discrete honeycombs of information. You could go stark raving mad just thinking of this, the crisscross, parallel lives of all of us, lives that don't quite touch but veer close anyway; lives that will go down like so much dust from a back porch, out of the carpet into the wild, ragged air. We were not meant to touch. We were meant only to stay in our cubicles and houses, never intersecting. We were compartmentalized, sequestered, removed from the sweat of each other. It all made bureaucratic sense. I would dive down deeply into a pool of blue water in my daydreams, and no one was there to greet me. Even our daydreams and fantasies were separate. So many things to insure, so many contingencies. I lived for a time in the great belly or furnace of the insurance industry, at the very nadir of its guts and turning, and its sheer vastness and intricacy stunned me.

This was the underworld of Omaha, "O-my-God" turning into "O-ma-ha," a place where awe is contained and filed away, electronically; a city where the angels of death swoop down transmogrified into dust devils from construction sites (small, brief tornadoes winding up to take off and disappear), the wheeling arcs of pigeons breaking into heartbreak from abandoned buildings. You wished for rain. You wished some days for anything to break the routine, the pattern. You wanted those small beads of water to add up to something on the windowpanes, something human, something you could contemplate for a while, discover in your sleep, add to the texture of your dreams. You wanted this rain to water plants you had not yet bought, seep down to the roots like slow terror and start the whole damn thing all over again: birth, life, and death, seeds in unsuspecting places, the origin of gasps and suffocation. Because the rain was free and you were not; because the voices on the magnetized tape were small clips of careful pronunciation, of cooperation with a power no one understood or witnessed; you wanted it to rain and beat on those windows—let me out, let me out—streaking your vision of outside, because what were you going to do when you went home? How were you going to live your life apart from this insurance, these small beads that touched the well of your own soul? In that office, in my cubicle, I came to realize the full horror of this city for the very first time; I felt like I was pickled in a jar of formaldehyde, as if each and every one of my senses was protracted to a point where they no longer registered real pain and joy anymore, a Kafkaesque and indefinite suspension of all flavors and sensations. I had fantasies of smashing things up, throwing a tizzy to prove I was human, breaking down, breaking away. Give me a blister and I will open it; give me a knife and I will throw it at a board. Give me the streets, the wind, the sky, and the alleys, the stink of garbage and the rooting of stray dogs; clear nights of stars, cold breezes, snow, rain, sleet, something hard and flinty against my face. Give me music and Chinese food, hustlers around the Greyhound bus terminal, sleeping rooms, the public library, a sheaf of poems, a hat, a boot, a rusty knife. Give me anything but this cubicle and the anonymous surface of this desk, mica-laden and crushing in the extreme, the insurance of anti-life in the midst of death, anti-beauty and anti-skin, anti-love in the great hierarchy of rational means.

II

When I left that job, it was like coming home for the first time. I was free, but how long would it last? I was still under that same sky, near those same buildings that were cleaned late at night or early in the morning. Omaha became destiny, then, as each patch of being was still an aspect of the sun that showed or didn't show but loomed horribly on the hotplate of the mind into tomorrow. Omaha: you come here because you can't help it, there's nowhere else to go. Omaha will take you, break you in slowly, make you love it and hate it as you love your own clothes. Omaha will nibble on your toes like a tadpole or grind you down into a different kind of dust. For the few, it is a place of covert liberation, a place to hide in public, uncover your true self. These are intimations only, gleaned from a lifetime of watching and listening. Why would you come here? Omaha is a good place to learn how to listen to music. Why would you stay here, sink down roots, start over, start over? Omaha is a good place to learn how to read. Why would you never come this way again, leave at all costs? Omaha is a good place to figure out what you want. Omaha is comfortable and nondescript, beautiful only because it stokes the imagination in reverse; you have to have imagination to live here or let it atrophy into dead muscle.

But the people who walk by these huge bay windows are my people, your people, any people who walk city streets anywhere in the world, chained to their wrist watches, schedules, or sexual demons; the wind blows more fiercely here, it is true, so their faces are bound to be bent somewhat in consternation and sobriety, leaning into the wind, holding on to their pocket holders and tulip hats. You want to touch them and not-touch them, like you would the fur of a slightly overweight dog; you want to know what makes them tick, the mystery of faces, even as you know these strangers are passing even now into another realm of namelessness. In Omaha the abiding mystery is wind funneled through alleys and tall buildings, scraps of blown newspaper, ruffled fur of the chained Irish setter. I watch, sip my coffee, bow to the brightness of the sun.

You hear rumors; you hear that people move here for the new technology fields out west in the suburbs, for the good schools and safe environment. You also hear how people (young people mostly) want to get the hell out and never come back, save for the holidays. To stay here, some think, is an admission of some kind of gray, diluted failure, a resignation to the small grinding gears of a modest midwestern city. "I'm from Omaha but . . ."; "You'd be surprised what Omaha has to offer"; "Omaha is a great place to raise kids"; "People are always surprised when they come to Omaha"; "Not bad for Omaha." Omaha, Omaha, Omaha: It sits in the mouth like a bland cherry that has lost all its flavor, an old, kindly uncle who comes around a bit too often, coughing up phlegm, smelling of furniture polish on threadbare shirts, pawing with quaking ease the rocks-glass full of Jack Daniels. Omaha is not a great city, in the sense of grandeur or history; it sits on the muddy Missouri like a car battery waiting to be sold, barely used, clean and dirty in equal amounts (shiny cover, soiled underparts), functional but woebegone outside the belly of its never-car. It would hum in the cadence of pure idling if only given a chance, the metaphysical humming that contains the mystery of all great cities: instead it lies inert, waiting, waiting, prey to the intensity (its one virtue) of every season.

Maybe people come here to lick their wounds, start over in a safer place, resign themselves to the small shallows of a place that will not mock them; maybe they come here because where they're from, Omaha is a big city, as big as they ever want to see, and so has its doses of seediness and vice; maybe they come because no one else will take them, they don't fit in in those other places for some reason, those small towns or the huge ones, the ones that demand they bow to the prevailing trends or perish somewhere down in scratching oblivion. Or maybe they come to Omaha because it is just the right size, not too big, not too small, and thus will accommodate any number of qualified desires: education, standard of living, low pollution, nice suburbs, ad infinitum, down to the scrubs of all reasons. They're tired, just tired, of competing with coastal America, tired, tired, tired, of the traffic and the crowds (though traffic here is getting worse); it's time to settle their bones down and experience the quiet, sustained dying this city will give them. For whatever reason they're here, they learn the embarrassed grace of apology, of qualifying all the characteristics of where they live—it's better than some places, worse than others—they die a thousand deaths comparing it to any other city. Omaha, in the very woefulness of the word, makes you gentler somehow, softer at the core. Because here the tides come in and go out with a deeper kind of base and gravity, time moves through you to either enrich your native force or destroy it slowly. Omaha. Let the word stay on your tongue like a slow-moving curse that kills by soft stings, or swallow it whole, the bile of knowing this is a strange place to die.

If you're from here, Omaha is alternately small beads of desperation that never break the skin and a safe haven of motherly smells, starched shirts and the woefulness of clean socks. And sitting here in this clean coffee shop, with spotless windows ten-feet high (no real walls in this place), I have come to think about this city and this sky and us below it here, these strangers who walk by, odd shapes you could not dream up in any fun-house sequence. They must have come here from somewhere. Wild hair of the inventor, shot glasses of the befuddled and almost blind Chinese boy with his seeing stick. These human and wind-blown tides are beyond my ken, I wonder what each of them might mean. Pigeons break and wheel in mysterious patterns behind an empty building (in Omaha, most buildings seem eerily empty), Pentecostal birds navigating their own kind of twilight resurrection. I see them in heartbreaking flight, wheeling arcs I cannot reckon with. In this downtown of glass and steel, you must learn to worship the sky because that's all there is. That, and the slow creeping forward of the sun. The sun could be your life measuring out its increments in slow inches, in shadows and great swaths of sun; you could live here and never seize your heart's greatest intent, which you come to know is a good thing and a bad thing. The city is lovely and ugly in turn, always changing faces like the god Janus. Today it is adamantine and brilliant, stripped clear of anything but sun and the grateful shade of tree-lined streets. I ride these tides almost daily, the tides between deep affection and slow suffocation, the counterpoint of self and place. I love this city because I can't help it, but I don't know if I'd come here from any other place.

At the top of the former Brandeis Building, gigantic tornado sirens sprout in hydra-headed wonder, the chorus of sounds you never want to hear that blare their warnings for tornadoes or bombs. You don't want to hear these wails, ever. You don't want to hear them cranking up at the first of each month in spring and summer, testing out their vocal chords for the imminent arrival of violent ghosts or fallout. I see these sirens almost every day. They are my first memory of this city, the first sight that made me realize that none of us is ever quite safe. What are they doing hundreds of feet in the air? Their mouths could swallow a body whole, gigantic fabricated bluebells, shatter your eardrums with the first wind-up and crank, blast you into craziness by the sheer breadth of their intensity and sweep. For if you are trying to reach a whole city, with people asleep in their beds or watching baseball on TV, or even to interrupt a domestic argument in a run-down kitchen, then you better court craziness and an artificial wail that has no corollary in nature—just one strident, unbelievably loud siren that booms over the fields and neighborhoods, maybe as far, it seems, as a bird call to Chicago. Who could stand under this wailing and take it? Who would want to? Who could bear even the sight of it from afar, belching forth that sustained whine that is ruination coming down like plague? Fitting that one of the highest points in the city is these alarum drums, high up and vigilant, criers of the most violent force in nature and in man. So we live under this vigilance, this artificial cry that could blot out any Mahler or acoustic guitar. God save us from this sound, this chorus of sound that weaves a crude melody of danger and ungodly winds. I watch the people walk by, I watch them stare ahead, battle the wind that always gathers downtown between the tall buildings, forming funnels of intense air, the current you lean into to get where you're going.

III

You come here because you're afraid. You come here to give up on your dreams. You come here to swaddle your pride in a new kind of blanket, one that will not rough up your skin. You come here because your husband left you and you have three kids, and this is a good place to work out your own version of salvation. You come here for snow, for solace, to take time out from more ambitious America, to love your dogs, to grow a vegetable garden, to find God, to admit your follies, to delude yourself further, to get in touch with the seasons. All of it must make sense here, in the middle of the country, Omaha, because it knows what heartbreak is, and heartbreak is steadfast and real, a thubbing kind of underwater pain, and this city will heal you over the years, take the edge off. They walk by me, so many channels or vectors of deep interior space, people counting off their duties, loves, horrors; and because I am from here, I claim the ultimate excuse—that this is where my first consciousness formed, where I scraped my knees on the blacktop, fell in love with so many girls, raced my brothers home on our bikes. This is where I first tasted rain and saw the queer char-treuse afterlight of a tornado. This is where I first heard those sirens so high up above, screaming in a swath of unbelievable sound. Omaha is the savage place in my heart, and the gentle corner. I am here for now. The sky is so much wandering, blues that exchange molecules for a different light and color. If you were here now, you'd probably fall in love with the sky and the possibilities of Highway 680 leading out of town, westward—you'd have to; you would hear the surf of rushing traffic that cuts through this city every day. And you might, too, feel the sense of possibility that many who live here also feel: the fleeting, heady, and impractical notion of following this sky wherever it might lead, but west, out of Omaha, out of O-Maha, that word that breaks the sadness to you one syllable at a time, until the last is the first echo of the best part of your heart, the unfinished business of dreaming.

Conducting Buses

P AT SLOBBERED because he could not help it, because his face was too big for his mouth, because his mouth was round and heart-shaped and always full of spit. He followed us around the neighborhood on an invisible leash, and his cheeks were small baskets of terror and glory. At forty he did not waste a second; any time he saw us he came loping after us, strings of saliva looping from his mouth like windswept gossamer. They were like threads of silk connecting him to this world. They were extravagant and long, as beautiful and shocking as any afterbirth. Slobber was the keynote of his character: it seemed to express both his desire and his need to communicate across his own body's water and gushing. He sopped up the constant stream by wiping the water away with a sleeve until the sleeve became a damp towel and his mouth a sudden brook or pond. His mouth was always wet. It was the fountain in himself he was always fighting, the source of impossible rushing and trickles that kept his sleeve close to his face like a shipwrecked sailor. He had sweet blue eyes in a pasty white face. Cowlicks stood up in his brown hair, as if he had been rubbing a balloon there all afternoon. He walked and limped, Humpty-Dumpty style, carrying his square body toward home.

Some days you could see him blocks away, coming up a hill and talking to himself. Then we scattered and hid. He was talking about buses and their various stops around the city. He had a penchant for schedules and addresses. "You live at 93rd Street, right? But not at 84th? Mrs. Abler lives on 84th; but you live on 93rd, right? I take the number 3 to 93rd, but I take the number 4 to 47th." This was the sum and total of his conversation; sometimes he would ring the doorbell and ask these questions again and again, never veering from numbers, streets, or buses. It was like he was working a groove so deep that only he could understand the patterns of living and dying; it was like he was trying to confirm the quadrants of his world so that he could hold them in place forever.

We used to run away when we saw him. We used to warn, "Pat is coming." That was enough to move us into giggling and hiding. "Pat is coming" was like saying that dread was coming, or a clown we didn't understand. It was inevitable, both funny and serious at the same time. Then we hid behind bushes or trees, watching his slow progress up the hill. He would come on then, fresh from the fluorescent tubes of the bus. Sometimes he would go from house to house, ringing doorbells and asking his water-bright questions. Some people took time to talk to him, others slammed the door, still others did not answer at all, until Pat knew an easy touch from a cold one and adjusted his routine accordingly. After years of this, he just walked home, hoping to come upon a hapless stranger.

Now it strikes me we were avoiding a person we didn't understand; his drooling and questions kept us safe from some unknown terror, maybe the terror of ourselves, or brought it up close to our faces. It's not that we made fun of him or didn't like him; we just didn't know what he was after, and yet there was something else going on. Behind his slobber and questions and long walk from the bus stop something odd and frightening was happening. It was a kind of reckoning, a little woebegone and savage, the coming on of fate. Even as kids we knew Pat was real, more real than any other person we saw that day. He was real because he could not fake his desires and panic. You sensed that his simple questions were his whole life, like he was trying to fend off doom. They took on the quality of a frantic prayer; nowhere in his limited lexicon did he ever try to be fancy or cute. He wanted facts and numbers, the implicit balm of exchange. It was a chant he was working toward, the relative permanence of things, not buses at all but patterns and people and how they lived by numbers. You could almost exchange, "Mrs. Abler lives on 93rd, right?" with "You are my friend, right? We will share this information together, right?" It was a little harrowing and breathtaking, a little like speaking over a gorge. To talk to Pat you had to be in the mood for the long haul, to give and give and repeat yourself, to let yourself love him.

You could see the number 2 bus drop him off, and see his slow ascent. You could see him working it out in his own mind while the rest of the world went about its business, wind or rain, cars and blowing newspapers. He was a lone figure gnawing on some deep internal bone, getting to the marrow of it by walking and muttering. Looking back on it now, I think of him as the only rooted being in that entire suburban landscape, so chained to a purpose and a cause that he had a gravity of one, so that I am surprised now that the sidewalk, trees, and street signs did not loose themselves and disappear into the atmosphere; or that everything else, mailboxes, flower beds, bird feeders, weren't that same stuff of deflection against a greater sense of doom that only he was aware of. Sometimes barn swallows swam around his head in ducking twos and threes. They seemed appropriate somehow. I can't prove it, but I think Pat was in touch with a kind of terror, the terror of not having anything to keep us rooted to each other.

This is a gift, though it took me many years to realize it. His cheeks would not let you go once they had grabbed hold of you. It was a good place to be for awhile, his cheeks; you knew you were safe there, never to be forgotten. And the slobber, too, was just a sloshing of memory or baptism. If you were nice to him, if you listened to his questions and answered, then you were his friend for life. More: you were part of his mind and water. You swam in his memory, his spittle and damp sleeve. He wouldn't let you go. He swallowed you, he held onto you, he recycled you in his juices. I think now that he was trying to canoe out of his own mouth into something simple and clear. Alone but not alone, safe yet vulnerable, his life seemed to me then one a channel widening out into a broad bay. All he had to live on were water, questions, and addresses.

A short time ago I saw him again for the first time in years; he had gained a little weight and his cowlicks were going gray. But leaving the bus he was the same, though slower now in movement. He was more thoughtful, less ravaged by numbers. I watched him from a red light. I thought of a symphony of buses and how he might conduct them from a super-raised podium. I saw his cowlicks on fire, and all the sparks and blazes of his blue eyes and waving arms; and I saw the water leaving his mouth in delicate tufts or waves, dripping over the soft petal of his lower lip, falling slower than serum or molasses into the unseen reservoir at his feet, the wet husk of his body held in rapture and wonder.

Light Calling to Other Light

LATELY, I HAVE STARTED to push a wide, yellow candle into sunlight, inching it forward on the coffee table at certain times of day. I move it forward to capture the light and to hold it for a while. Then its entire fat body glows from within in a rich, mellow flame, like an improbable, headless Buddha who is dining on the universe. Aglow on the table, it is an homage to light for light's sake. It never fails to astonish me. And this same candle, which is squatty and well abused, thick enough to lap your knee, could burn for a long, long time, though I rarely deign to light it. I move it into sunlight inches at a time and by late afternoon, the tallow is warm and bright. Then girth becomes a virtue; you wish it were thicker, fatter, more encompassing of sun, wider than the circumference of a saucer. So one day I discovered its true virtue and have been its devoted slave ever since. Prostrate, a little shabby and banged about at the rim, the outer edges of the candle create a daytime aura the nimbus of which is good enough to chew on.

And so I have started to collect tiny scraps of light. I have been collecting them, I realize now, all of my life. I put them in an imaginary bag the size of a small yard that, when closed before I go to sleep, collapses to a hand-held pouch. I put the stars of new snow in that bag, glistening like bits of glass or diamonds; dawns over the Platte River, the water keen at the knife's edge where it meets the sun. Then I'm a woebegone sucker, staring at the auroras of other places, holding on to what I know not. I also collect the transparent wings of small birds, hummingbirds whirring at a feeder, coloring the air behind them in the delicate, purple lattice of a bruise; waving grass off the highway that shines in early afternoon (it does shine if the wind is right); the perfect rib cage of venetian blinds in early morning, which hardly bends at all but *cuts down into* the nadir of things; the sun again through branches of the gingko tree, wild hair of the weeping mistress, bands of winter cirrus above them.

I collect these scraps of light for a reason I do not know or understand. I cannot define it. They are props against heedlessness and a certain kind of waste. I need these scraps of light very much, for without them I am much reduced in my capacity to deal with my own pettiness and cruelty—and that of others.

But the scraps of light are destructive, too, if a balance is not achieved. When the winter sun is going down, and I feel I alone am there to watch it among my own exhalations, I know that it is light calling to other light. It is the crisp majesty of such cold and brightness that restores my belief in something else, even if it is just winter brightness for winter's sake. Light calling to other light, summer bogs, different kinds of churning water, shafts of yellow sunlight, each color, band of day—is this what we have, finally, to look forward to? Is this what we are meant to achieve by awe and recognition? The bag could unfold, burst into flames. Best not to stoke this fire too much. Best not to gaze directly at it, best not to wonder too hard at the need behind its growing collection, the recognition of tallow made from skin, hair and eyes, the inflammatory nature of desire.

Once when I was a boy I couldn't get my tennis shoes on fast enough. My mates were outside, calling for me to join them. I was in the basement among spokes and wires of sunlight; they came down at angles from the cellar windows, dazzling beams that slanted across the room and my body. The stairs, too, were blazing with autumn sun, vectors of light that showed the dance of dust motes in their wake like small galaxies. I couldn't tie my shoes fast enough, I almost whimpered. I have never been this happy before or since, this charged with *the moment*, this animal and this divine. I was humming, vibrating with light, like that same candle or thin reed on fire. The light fell across my trembling hands. I wanted to run, run, run all day. The light was all around me, the light was inside me, too.

Czesław Miłosz says that certain moments in childhood are like sacraments that we draw on later in life. We have them so that later, when we are adults and not quite so sure of who and what we are, life tumbling all around us, we can turn to these for solace and for hope. I think he is right. I think we all have these moments — and they are suffused with light that is both internal and external, light calling to other light. That moment in the basement was a sacrament of light, trembling and unallayed joy, and I ran up that staircase of light into another light — and now I am humbled, afraid, and grateful all at once. I answered the call of my fellows, I ran out to greet them before the sun ended our play.

One night a few years ago at the end of October all the trees in the neighborhood started to groan and buckle under the burden of heavy, wet snow. They lamented and came apart all night. Blue sparks popped from transformers, power lines went down in heaps, and black snakes writhed with the voltage of God in them. I didn't sleep all night. Sheer weight and groaning were doing the trees in. The next morning all the streets were impassable with downed trees, and people came out of their houses, blinking at the wreckage in dumbfounded wonder. Trees that were once vertical were now horizontal and mangled. Streets were unrecognizable mazes, zigzags of footprints in new snow. Our building was without power for three days. And in that sudden winter darkness our own home became a place of coldness and dread; we watched the sun go down with misgiving, we gathered in public places lit up by generators. We put our faith in candles and each other. The candle became purely functional, we clung to its girth and its wide circumference of warmth. At night we studied the flame and each other. I hung out at my neighbors' telling stories, sharing candles. It was a sudden, atavistic return to simple fire, and we crowded around the candles like pilgrims. How many months, years had we avoided this need; how had we put off the calling of fire for other kinds of artificial light; how had we avoided a reckoning with our own need for sun. The hallways of our building were blackest night, even in broad daylight. You had to carry your candle or flashlight wherever you went, hand cupped around the flame.

When the power finally came back on, I was walking up the hill with two neighbors. Most of the neighborhood was still dark, dormant hellmouths looming. When we rounded that street corner and saw all those windows full of light, we laughed and cheered. We were suddenly more conscious than before of our own needs. We thanked each other for our company. We walked toward those lights with a new awareness. And even now I think of that sudden spike of joy, that simple switch between gloom and the bright snap of home. Because the homes we had were not really homes without light. We knew that then. They were places to avoid until we had to go to sleep, preternatural tombs. But now they were honeycombs of brightness, and we went toward them willingly, a little surprised, I think, at our own emotions, which were somewhere between gratefulness and sorrow that the long darkness was finally over.

I reach into the bag for a window sill, clean scrape of light like a board across it, white glowing with dust. For no reason at all I level it to my nose and inhale. The bag contains a catalogue of the world and its different shades and brightnesses, membrane of the jellyfish, my niece's glowing hands. Sometimes the page I'm reading in the morning is bright like the flashing scales of a snake, and I cannot read the words. But I am loathe to draw the shades. If I cannot read for those few seconds or minutes I must be reading something else, the sudden cursive and cups of light that radiate all things around me.

In a dream once I saw the translucent wings of a sea gull banked against the sun. It screeched out to me or to no one. And as the sea gull passed from that outer rim of light, I was suddenly there, too, in the bird's wings, holding the stitches in place against the oncoming fire. Wheeling, circling, the sea gull was trying to show me something, circle of light I could never touch. The sea gull is deep in the bag.

When my neighbor looks at me, she who is now ninety-four, I see in her eyes that same sea gaze and steadiness of purpose; she looks through me and doesn't even mean to do so. She shuffles in her tiny, painful steps. But it is those eyes, her light, that plummets me sometimes to the bone toward another region where there is no age or time as we know of it.

Now I cast out my bag of light, a net unraveling in space. Here is what tumbles out in the star-touched wreckage: eyes everywhere, small valleys of shadow in footprints of snow, neon strobe of the radio tower in a blizzard, broken glass in the vacant lot where there is no other beauty, glowing seeds near the city park bench, pigeons on fire and clucking all around those same seeds, ripple of light in the moving branches of the sycamore whose bark is peeled white high up in the branches. Here is my random sample of these scraps of light that sustain me for reasons I do not know, the reflex of opening the blinds each morning, craning my neck toward the east, walking in the sun without sunglasses. We are light calling for other light, and these lights come careening from all angles, we cannot stop them. And I collect these scraps of light. I collect them so that when it is late or the bad news keeps coming, I can put my wrists right through them to the elbow and let them hold me for awhile.

Light calling to other light, splendor of the sun-blanched stone, we close our eyes to the sun so that other, less blinding suns may enter and we can gather them and give them away when the brightness is too much; or when the candle, which is even now slumbering in latent heat, may reach out of the bag and hold me in a calm embrace in the duration of the sun passing from morning into darkness.

Rex and Cleopatra

The Sign

SHE WALKS A FEW STEPS behind her companion in the cold, bright morning when it is only ten degrees and she is without hat or mittens. She takes baby steps, careful over the icy sidewalk, as the rail-thin, mousy man in front of her talks loudly to himself and gestures toward the sky. They are a pair, these two. He is leading her to a secret promised land, a cabala of the privileged few, though no one but they can see or understand it. They wear second-hand clothes, cheap jackets and shirts, grimy tennis shoes and flimsy windbreakers, not at all fitted out for this bitter weather. They have no scarves or hats. I don't know how they put up with this cold. I don't know where they go each morning, but the circuit always leads them back this same way. I keep waiting for them to take the season into account and clothe themselves properly. But each day they pass by my apartment window, the same ill-kept and eccentric passersby, she with her Styrofoam cup of coffee and exposed fingers and he with his strange, loud proclamations sent roughly skyward.

I have come to wait for them to appear, doomed to the exact paces of each other, regimented strangers who are familiar now in their rounds. I have come to admire their heedlessness of weather and everything else, except the queer intensity they carry inside them. They are so serious it is both breathtaking and laughable, out of proportion with these drab working-class streets. They walk them as if they are following a thin thread of life with stern, twisted faces out of all proportion to the small houses around them.

Maybe I am ready for these prophets, though they need not yell at me. Maybe I am ready for them to lead me past the wilderness of my own heart. I know that the hidden worlds they speak of are real, though

I cannot prove it. I know they are on a singular track. Why she follows and he leads I am not sure; but I think they share a secret in a tongue no one else can speak. I see them wandering, peripatetic, like two pilgrims on their way back from a Fata Morgana where the face of God is the face of a kitten or a billboard of smiling newscasters with two-foot teeth. Not quite out of their minds, they are moving slowly out to another perimeter—and I follow them from a safe distance, a voyeur behind the slats of a venetian blind.

Last week I saw a woman I had not seen for years, in a neighborhood market; she looked greatly changed in the bright aisles of the grocery store, a little woebegone, disheveled, a crumpled heap of what she used to be. Her face was caved in and her hair was matted, and I thought I saw a palsy in her movement, a slight quivering that shook a can of beans. I turned away. I think she saw me, though I am not sure. I was unshaven, disheveled myself: more and more I go out not caring how I look. We were a match, the two of us, Frick and Frack, a shadow perhaps of our former selves, wrecked on purpose or indifference in a grocery store. I thought right away of the eccentric neighborhood tandem, whom I shall call Rex and Cleopatra: we could be understudies for them, follow in their footsteps, only she would lead and I would follow. It seems a wholesome possibility. But this woman in the grocery store used to be quite brilliant, and, in her way, a lovable pain in the behind: she told you what she thought whether you liked it or not. In fact, she was extraordinarily combative and confrontational. She was smart and knew it, and she threw her knowledge at you like a weighted rope spangled with fishhooks. I heard she had a breakdown and spent a few weeks in Richard Young. I heard they strapped her down in a gurney and delivered a few slugs of sedative. This was after she opened her own theater in town. She used to smoke three packs a day and cackle and laugh her way through the hallways of the English department where we both taught briefly, she as an adjunct and I as a graduate assistant. She liked me, I think, because I looked up to her. Other people, men mostly, called her a "bitch on wheels," "Lady Macbeth," and "Lady Godiva." I noticed they always did this behind her back, in hushed tones, looking over their shoulders. I got a kick out of the intrigue until she grew so angry at the appalling, old-boy climate that she told the chair off and stormed out of this particular department forever, leaving a few drifting pages and red-hot ears in her wake.

But that was years ago: now look at us, suddenly, looking for bargains and ducking each other between the aisles. Life has turned out differently than we planned. "The innocent and the damned" she used to call us: we got a kick out of that in the old days. But now I could not bring myself to talk to her, though I kept her in the corner of my eye. Her glasses were so thick they looked like bullet-proof glass, distorting the true color of her eyes. Where before she had carefully groomed, short red hair, like Annie Lennox, now it was chopped up, longish, with stray wisps like dirty strands of broom sticking out from a floppy winter hat. What happened to you, Cathy? What pushed you to the glass edges of your nerves? She seemed like she had lost a few inches in height, and her face was creased and puffy at the same time, like a volleyball that had been deflated and pumped up too many times. If I had not known her, she would have been just another shrinking figure on the border of recognition, a flicker that registers once and goes away, one of those indigent or impoverished souls who push their foodstuffs all the way home in rickety carts. Her sweater was too big for her, and the sleeves hung hollow and drooping like a judge's robe. Only her eyes burned with a peculiar fire, though the focus and intensity I remembered were now diminished, warped into a passive blue smoking among the canned goods. They glowed in a weird half-life that looked like the phosphorescent sheen of run-off.

Seeing her, imagining myself in her eyes, shocked me into realizing that none of us are safe, not even if we have a fine and delicate mind; sometimes this can collapse too for no apparent reason. Here was the future, looking out at us, and we fairly scurried away from each other. I saw her leave the store and stare ahead into a vacancy I couldn't see, as her dirty hat bobbed pathetically on her head like the body of a skinned rabbit.

The Revelation

Now it is 4:30, and Rex and Cleopatra are retracing the steps they had taken only hours before. Still he leads by the twitch and tremble of his ratty mustache, and Cleo is having some trouble again on a patch of ice. Where do they live? Where do they go? They wear the same clothes day after day; their hair has that same unwashed quality. Maybe they have no comb. Maybe their comb is their own fingers, wetted with their tongues. Maybe they share a mattress or a box spring or a couch seared with cigarette burns.

But how unaccountably relieved I am that they show up again, walking their way through the debris of their own skulls. How appropriate they now seem for everything else that has gone wrong over the years: they are not fictional characters or salesmen but flesh and blood individuals with grease stains on their jackets. I promise you that. They rattle their spare change in their pockets, thinking of their next meal. They share something beyond camaraderie. Suddenly, inexplicably, I am glad they found each other. I hope Rex continues to rave his head off for years to come in the frozen land of the downtrodden, his loyal, mittenless companion behind him. I hope he never cares what people think of him. He has something to say and he will say it. And Cleo is pulling up the rear, following in the wake of his words, holding her gift of coffee, looking over the edge of her tennis shoes.

We take odd characters in, rework them, project our own clean and sullied lives upon them. This is beyond empathy: for some reason a gesture, posture, or stoop takes us in, and we suddenly find ourselves thinking of torn fingernails, dirty socks, a coupon good for a cup of coffee. It's a ruthless manipulation. Rex is subdued this time, though his mouth is forming words I cannot hear. Cleo's hands disappear inside the sleeves of her light jacket. I see both of their breaths unfurl before they vanish like the distant ringing of a bell.

My ex-father-in-law once saw a couple of dirty homeless kids in the rain in San Francisco. He told me he will never forget their faces, or his regret at not stopping and giving them a few twenty dollar bills. He regrets this and thinks about them once in a while. But the bigger question is, Why those two? Why not the countless others who dot our landscape, why kids with body piercings and hoops through their noses? "They couldn't have been more than fifteen," he said; and he says it with the same kind of horror and pity, as if he cannot believe they were there in the first place, as if he had seen deer in the middle of a busy street, or a panda juggling dishes. He says it as if they had broken wings or some freakish trait that defies ordinary human characteristics, horns planted in their foreheads or bodies without limbs. He wanted to help them and now they are gone forever; they have left him haunted without their ever having seen his face. "I wish I had stopped for those kids"—and he is a brusque man, rude to waiters, dictatorial, used to getting what he wants, silk shirts and martinis mixed just so. His reaction to two homeless children in San Francisco is out of proportion to anything he evinced before or since, but they . . . they continue to have a hold on him.

You can't tell me the world is a straightforward place, that our actions and reactions make sense, that even the love we feel for our own has any correlation whatever to the way gravity works or the revolution of the stars. We love and hurt for no reason at all—or something beyond reason that words or meaning cannot touch.

I have seen Rex and Cleopatra so many times that it is only now that they are finally starting to take hold, turning me inward, forcing me to ask what they mean by the sheer inertia of their habits. They have bloomed in my mind's eye like the most improbable of flowers. I am now conscious of them, wait for their passage and disappearance. Before they were almost a part of the street, like debris that sticks around for awhile. Only now do I wonder what the hell they are up to, day after day, as the year gets darker and colder. Why the sudden gaze into the motivations of others when they will not avail their reasons to me now or ever? It is not my place to know, never was: nonetheless, they stick with me, haunt me somehow. I can't help but feel they are trying to tell me something, and I can't figure out what it is. This is their life in Omaha, and it is a serious, biblical affair.

I will make you small among the nations, you shall be utterly despised. The pride in your heart has deceived you, you who live in the clefts of the rock, whose dwelling is high, who say in your heart, "Who will bring me down to the ground?" Rex yells outside my window, ad libbing his garbled, twisted oaths around this, and the circle continues to collapse, a ripple of air and energy folding in on me, and I am pinpricked by the few words I understand; I am pinpricked more by what I do not understand, disturbed, perplexed, looking for reasons in the straight paths of this prophecy.

They are likely to strike me or yell at me if I intervene; the closest I can get is right here, right now—and the present moment could be woefully way off in resembling any real truth or purpose. I must remember that. I must remember that they have nothing to do with me. I could be fooling myself right now, to be taking them so seriously. But I do not think so. A crow flies up, wings hoofing, and Rex stops a moment to shake his fist at the sky. Cleopatra pulls up the rear, stopping a full three yards behind him in mincing steps. Who knows what it means. Who would come here if they knew, who would cradle the delicate Styrofoam of warm liquid and wait for the words, oaths, and shaking to stop, the tremors of a man with the proportions of a broom; who would wait in the cold morning catching a whiff of death in the chill of her own hands; or curse a blackbird for being itself; who is no longer afraid of what they could become if something, anything, leaned on them too hard?

Because we are here, we watch TV and buy each other gifts at Christmas time. We sip our wine or coffee and go to bed. Rex and Cleopatra will continue to walk their strange, thin line near the precipice of a canyon only they can see. And one day we will be cold, too, in the dark morning. We will make peace or division with the sudden specter of who and what we really are, and it will take our breath away as the false worlds fall into the gutter.

Listening to Mahler

L ATE SUMMERS in Nebraska are thick with the weight of intrusion. Crickets cry out all night in steady, clicking notes, the rising and falling hum of an invisible chain that makes you realize none of us is ever truly safe. I sleep in front of a fan, panting like a dog. The night sounds are almost on top of me in the room, in the bed, in my own patches of damp that gasp for air like moist sand over my shoulder blades. Some nights I wake in a panic, vaguely wet and out of breath. I go to the window to breathe. Outside, fireflies strobe by in their soft green lights, conveying messages of some prehistoric doom, and I feel that I have landed here on this earth as a mistake: I was not made for this kind of late summer lushness.

And what I claim tonight is a small thing that suddenly looms large on hot summer nights when I can't sleep; what is mine is smaller than the phosphorescent glow of those same fireflies, barely enough to light them up for two more seconds. What I claim is the sudden memory of waking hours before dawn to work at UPS loading package cars (we could not call them trucks) at 3:30 A.M., sweating as soon as I stood on the belts and faced the revolving metal cage that lapped your area every two minutes on a huge conveyor belt, chock-full of packages, tires, shovels, small trees — a cornucopia of shipped goods whose destinations and addresses you memorized by where they fit in the package car.

I think of my former coworkers, those who work even now as I stand here breathing in the night air (it's 3:00 A.M.), how tired they must be now after all these years, how hard they still work past the aching of tired bones, child support, other jobs, night class, some of their wrists laced up for carpal tunnel in sweat-stained jackets. They're still there—and I'm here, restless but free. I think of them at moments like these, when I can't sleep late at night; I think how lucky I was to get away, to escape, to move on to other work that does not require sweat and a sore back. But I can still hear the din of the center and smell the exhaust of leaving trucks. I can still close my eyes and hear the great dynamo of the belts in full swing, an insect kind of place where the grinding work and repetition made you numb to almost any kind of mercy, even for yourself. During the summer months we used to take strips of clear tape and hang them from the fluorescent lights above our belt; four hours later they would be peppered with mosquitoes and flies. You could see the insects fly in a frenzy above these lights, as madcap as any shower of huskless sparks. They zeroed in on the tape and your skin like they were trying to needle you with some kind of sharp and disturbing information, to reform your life, reform your life. You could count the furor of the day by the number of dead insects you had on the tape, a strange measure of the transparency of tiny death all around you. Those belts were not the place for false comfort or solace. But some of the loaders have worked at UPS for twenty years or more, seeing brown in their sleep. They're locked in until retirement, their bodies a patchwork of chronic problems always getting a little worse, backs and hands bent or bowed now by the incessant repetition of lifting and sorting. They have no clear ponds under their fingernails, no way to stop the ravages of early morning time.

I think of Mary, a woman with four kids, as cantankerous, ornery, and reliable as a one-eyed mule; she used to tell supervisors off regularly, threaten to notify the Teamsters for the smallest infraction (she was lifetime union). Her body was shaped like a banged-up accordion, squatty and strong. When I worked there she had already been with UPS for twenty-two years, getting tougher each year like a leather hide left out in the sun. But some days she brought in Swedish meatballs in a huge steaming crock, feeding us during our precious fifteen minute break. We gobbled up her meatballs like they were popcorn, the hot tangy sweetness like forgiveness on our tongues. Gray wisps flayed out from her temples like spider webs, and her thick glasses magnified her shrewd brown eyes that alternated between righteous fury and dangerous calm. I think she liked me because I was afraid of her and got her to tell stories.

Then there was Rick, the cellist and music teacher who gave private lessons at home; Rick had fourteen kids and was a born-again Christian who had written a book entitled *A Quiver Full of Arrows*, whose message was the bounty and necessity of large families. He is the only person I knew down there who never got upset, one of the happiest people I have ever known. In twenty years of work he missed only one day due to illness.

Some days we'd be sent down to unload trailers of packages outside of our area, and he and I would talk passionately about music as we toppled mountains of packages onto the rollers. Even in the hot, claustrophobic space of a semi-trailer—where the temperature could reach 140 degrees, trailers baking like ovens from the night before— we could escape the limitations of our jobs and our lives and rise just for a moment into the ether of music, discussing why Bartók turned to folk songs and Brahms played in burlesque parlors as a youngster; we could, for a moment, share the possibilities of music, and it lifted us out of the stifling morning into another time and place. When Rick used to talk about Mahler, he would roll his eyes skyward in some kind of strange relief and sigh, saying "Mahler" as if it were the word "tenderness" in some forgotten Germanic tongue.

For a few minutes each morning before our shift began, we would talk about what we listened to on the drive into work, a gift before fury. Even though it was ridiculously early, and work lay ahead like a penance, the twenty-minute drive from midtown to south Omaha was the best part of the day: no matter how tired you were, you could still lower your window at 3:00 A.M., drink in the lonely freeways, listen to the all-night classical station, and, for a moment, be fully alive in the summer night. The city parks and their empty swings could move you for no reason at all, or the dark alleys between buildings and their sweet whispers of corruption and garbage. Music flowed through you, you were Sibelius or Bach or the violin of a Beethoven sonata, or even the calm voice of the night announcer—the loneliest man in the world—a man so sad and intimate you thought he was speaking just to you. I learned to love his voice, to imagine his melancholy face and gray hair, and the way his spotted hands grabbed his ceramic mug, a slight tremor in the pond of his coffee. You thought you were the only listener in the world, and that the music he played betokened a hushed and sacred world where even the bats stopped beating their lovely leather wings.

Sometimes I used to drive downtown and take an alternate route on 24th, and I'd see a lonely prostitute or two shining sadly in their polyester tights and spiked high heels that lifted them above the sidewalk. I'd see the small orange glow of their cigarettes in the shadows, and I'd try to look at them eye to eye, to show them I was not afraid of the commerce of sex or of my own racing heart. We were connected somehow, and the connection was not lurid. For just a moment before I passed, the dark underworld of Omaha made some kind of human sense; each of us in our work paid the price of our own bodies, though they were out in the street, subject to danger and all kinds of violation, the hidden, dark flowers of corruption. Seeing them was somehow both noble and heartbreaking; maybe, in some part of the world, it didn't have to be this way. I'd drive by the prostitutes, hoping to see them, hoping to show them I was one man who wouldn't stop. And the shift from this world—of watching the run-down neighborhoods off 24th fly by in their woebegone shanties, the early morning sky replete with polished stars, trees pregnant and waiting, the freeway lights strobing their chalk-white veil, the announcer's sad voice and his lonely violins—all of this could almost, almost, make the whole damn thing worth it, your aching bones and the mind-numbing shift ahead of you. Music got you through it, lifted you above it, even if it was just for a note or two. You could somehow face the day ahead of you, the early hours of drudgery, and maybe even the rest of your life. Rick told me that he set his alarm clock to this same classical station. The alarm would go off, playing music, and he would lie in the dark for a few moments before he rose.

I imagine Rick in his dark, quiet house, all fourteen of his children asleep. I see him sit at the edge of the bed, motionless, letting the hushed music slowly bring him to wakefulness, perhaps wondering just how he arrived here at this moment in time and space, with all these kids and the womanly shape of his cello sitting in the corner, lady-in-waiting. I can see him wipe his wire-framed glasses, take a deep sigh, turn to the rustle of his wife turning over in sleep, utter under his breath "Dear God," and get up to do it all over again. This is the miracle, after all: that people like Rick and cantankerous Mary keep getting up and coming back for more, that they take pride in what they do, that loading packages and listening to music in the middle of the night is not just routine but a rhythm sounding at the deepest part of their lives. You could go your whole life loading forty-pound boxes of chocolate and not know this. You could go your whole life being overwhelmed by music in the middle of the night and not understand why. You could rise in the dark like a withered husk and face a terrible consciousness, that now, finally, this is all there is — this is your life, and you must deal with it. You must put in your twenty-five years, buy orthopedic shoes, suffer back surgeries, work your body into such a groove that even on Sundays you still wake up at 4:00 A.M. You could do all of this, slowly or fast, the realization and the resignation. But above it and through it always, for people like Rick, there is music somewhere coming from a tiny place, the cracked FM radio in his battered van, and you would know that only this music could take you forward and take you home.

I stand at the window and wish for rain. In some passages of Mahler, passages that have become hard-wired into my nerves, his chorus is singing in plaintive time of the songs of earth. My songs of earth, like Rick's or Mary's or anyone else's, play quietly at night when I can't sleep. They come out of the teeming of crickets. They sound, like the prostitute's quick drag of a cigarette before dawn, somewhere between hopefulness in the form of smoke and the sustained exhalation of everything we will ever be, fading into the dark like the last notes of a cello ceasing its poor rain of strings.

Opera of Trouble

Overture

I SAT IN THE LAST ROW of the balcony at the English National Opera, my mind spinning at the cathedral of air around me, as row upon row of seats wound like the inlaid filigree of a conch shell. I felt, then, that I was at the very top of the civilized world. I felt that I had landed here purely by accident, thrown down by a whim, and the shock and delight of it didn't diminish once all night, as I looked at the people below and around me, all of us transported here from places equidistant to desire. If I reached out, I thought I could touch the ceiling of the gilded dome. Only later would I realize that this world where I sat in wonder masked still others unknown to me, which would suddenly loom up out of the darkness of the city night, real and frightening worlds, as the screens that held them together fell away one by one. The opera was *Faust*, and it was my first brush with a world that would change everything. The lights dimmed and a hush came over the audience, and I was just one among the newly converted and watching eyes, waiting for something to happen.

Earlier that day I had come from the airport and jumped on the Tube, a twenty-two-year-old kid from Nebraska; I didn't care where it was going or where I would end up, just so long as I could move through the dark innards of London and watch the flashing stations go by like the spinning reels of memory or sickness. I wanted to be lost and not know where I was, to be carried away on rails that shook me from all I had ever been. I took to the streets without plan or destination. I didn't know anyone. What I wanted, looking back now, was experience, though it did not yet have a name; what I wanted were the rocking lights of the Tube taking me in the direction of night, out and away to the old boroughs. What I wanted was to be lost, among urban characters who didn't know me and staggered home drunkenly at night, or walked by hurriedly, lost in the habitation of their own secret selves. I wanted so much that it didn't have a name or a reason — only streets I had never walked, leading to open markets and cobbled bridges in Camden Town, and voices touched by centuries of history and fate that led, improbably, back to my own family's doorstep in Omaha. Those same streets and voices led me by chance to the gallery of an opera house, thousands of miles away from all I had known. Suddenly there I was.

This is not a new story, nor is it cause for any particular kind of celebration. I was just another young pilgrim in an exotic and foreign land. London was a city of sounds for me. And these sounds that rose out of the darkness were nothing I had ever heard before; they came out of the pit like longing itself and the turbulence of my own unformed heart, aching in the sudden pull of strings. This is not a new story, but an old and beautiful one, for I realized in that moment that I had been waiting my whole life, all twenty-two years of it, for just this moment to come out of the darkness of a theater and claim me. Where had I been all my life? Where had these performers been, and these faces around me staring out onto the stage lights to this other world where we all gathered alone and together? It was a hoop of desire I had suddenly passed through, and it left me feeling thwacked on the wrists and ankles. Faust was the first ticket into different regions of myself. I saw the conductor wave his hands over a small basket of light, and I knew then that I was suddenly different.

Faust came out in his black cape, hands held behind his back. He was thinking through his life, and he found it wanting and stale. The tenor playing the part was a small man, with wire-rimmed glasses and close-cropped blond hair. He strode around the stage as if he was reconsidering all of his assumptions, working them out among the footlights. His books were dry sticks, and he paced around the stage like a restless soul suddenly wanting to flee his whole life. Faust sang out in his anguish and pain for something else to fill his human cup; and Mephistopheles, materializing out of a thin puff of smoke with his staff and long, diabolical beard, promised fulfillment in the deep bass notes of temptation; and the dark faces around me, looking out onto the same stage—all of them wove themselves into a fabric of that strange night. I gripped the felt armrests and held on, waiting for Marguerite to appear, carried to another place where fear and consequence were replaced by the notion that everything from now on was possible, if only I could conceive of it in my head. I was waiting for Marguerite, too. I knew (or thought I knew) exactly what Faust was feeling. Even if I didn't understand the words, the music formed a bridge between my ignorance and the story; the music *was* the story. All I had to do was listen. By that time I had no choice anyway: I sat aching from grandeur through three hours of opera, barely moving. That this moment has never happened to me before or since only confirms the clarity of it: we can't reclaim anyway our first initiation into the world of music and trouble. It lies beyond the pale of recovery, an unredeemable gift given only once—and in that finitude we find ourselves somewhere we were not before, grasping for our new selves among the broken shards of the past. Youth, like a kind of blinder or cataract, is cast off and gone forever.

Later I walked out into the London streets into a nightmare of over-turned cars and gutted store fronts, among dark, angry faces and lakes of shattered glass. I walked straight into the aftermath of the 1990 Poll Tax riots of London like a sleepwalker suddenly awake in the troubled world—from the plush seating and safety of dreams into a hellmouth of social reality—and there was no healing salve or buffer between them, only vandalism and uncertainty, divided by thin walls that were crumbling all around me. I walked over broken glass lightly, carefully, as it shone brilliantly in the night like ice on black water, and tried to figure out what swirl of events brought me here to the brink of under-standing, suddenly so close to opera and social unrest that there were no longer any distinctions between them. What were opera and music compared with this? Nothing explained the breathtaking contrast be-tween the world of opera and the world of smashed glass just outside its doors, and the figures stealing all around me something for their future, the furtiveness of malevolence and rage. It was suddenly as if on a whim Mephistopheles had come outside to cast his spell of temp-tations over the city itself, and all of London had answered the dark prayers; I had been hoodwinked: opera was not real and this was. I walked faster and faster into the night, while people ran all around me looting and laughing, shouting dark oaths into the air above London. Two helicopters circled Trafalgar Square, casting their beams of light in sweeps of crisscrossing rays, while the overture to Gounod's *Faust* played in my ears. Figures ran past me, holding bricks, metal pipes, pamphlets, bottles; whistles shrilled; I heard Cockney voices yell obscenities at random, bottles smash.

Was I invisible to them, a young American who had hardly ever been out of the Midwest? Whose side was I on anyway? What *were* the sides? Someone jumped on the hood of a small car, rocking it back and forth, yelling something about foreigners. I couldn't understand what they were saying, even if they were using the English of my ancestors. I clutched my program and walked away from the epicenter of destruction as fast as I could, head down, just trying to get away. The whole city was dark and threatening.

"Where you from?" a man asked me urgently from nowhere, grabbing my sleeve. He held papers or documents; his bald head gleamed like chrome. I didn't know what he wanted me to say. "America," I said, and he let me go. "Fucking foreigners," he said, and walked away. He said it sweetly, as if caressing the epithet. I didn't know if it was a curse or a compliment—he seemed to mean it both ways. "I thought you were fucking Swedish," he said again, and laughed, moving away into the darkness where a mob gathered. I kept my head down, eyes open, feeling vaguely guilty for something I couldn't name, and heard the stampede of feet and shouting. Sirens boomed from indistinct sources, resolving themselves into alleys and fading away. I walked all the way to the flat in Camden Town through a small blizzard of trash and blowing newspapers, with *Faust* and the muffle of helicopters racing in my head.

Aria

I sing of a time before I knew what any of it meant, the collection of daydreams, tiny notebooks where I jotted down ideas, impressions, bad poems: I thought maybe I could make a story of this. I sing of memory that distorts and clarifies the first moments I knew I was alive, truly, achingly alive—those moments in the great city where the spires of buildings and ledges near Goodge Street brought me to myself. I thought I belonged there more than any other place I had ever been; I thought London was my true home. I would be proven wrong; but only after days and weeks just wandering the city alone, getting to know its scattered pigeons, its city sounds and the smells of damp and soot. I would go home to the Midwest and come back only in memory, like now, when I think I finally have some idea of what it was all about, this old story of wandering only to come full circle back to oneself, of coming to terms with the finitude of being in the dark, flashing caves of the Tube. I sing of selfishness that finally became myself, the old song of awakening. I sing of staring out train windows on day journeys from Victoria Station into the English countryside, watching the drab outskirts of London and the ragtag of laundry hanging like the patchwork of despair from tenement windows; of bad poems I thought at the time were good; of a silence so deep within myself I couldn't share it with anyone else. I sing of copying poems down from the rocking walls of the Tube, of staring for hours onto the Thames from the great bay windows of the Royal Festival Hall, trying to make the skyline a part of me always so that when I did return to the States I could call on that vision in times of doubt and trouble (I was there, I was there—here I am now); of calling my parents from under a bridge somewhere near that same great river, falling into that old role I thought I had banished for good; I sing of the privilege of travel that a dead relative I had never met—a woman who spent much of her life in an institution—had given me, of who she was, of what she looked like; now a month rarely goes by that I do not think of her and her largesse thrown into the future, my future, and it remains one of the keynotes of grace in my life; I sing of friends whose faces are still with me only in memory, fading with the years, half-formed faces because I never took a photograph in London; of plays and symphonies and galleries I sat through hungrily, storing it all up for a lifetime because I knew somehow that I would never be this free again; I sing of trash and alcohol and Alex, the Frenchman I met in an underground zinc bar in Soho, who scribbled his parents' address in Paris for me to visit if I ever went to France; I sing of a little old woman at Highgate Cemetery named Nora, who showed me how to clean and care for the gravestones of the dead when I volunteered for a month, as she led me down cobbled paths by the eerie arabesques and wisps of her white, white hair; and the snow-drops she taught me to love simply by pointing out their small white blossoms among the wet, granite slates and vines. I sing of looking out a three-story window at London University, not paying attention to the instructor but watching the pigeons and slant of light in the damp London morning off the angles of buildings. (I thought, then, that I would never see such beautiful angles again.) I sing of the Portuguese man in the school cafeteria who collected my change day after day, and our soft conversations about this or that. He told me his country was beautiful, and I could almost see the coast and the fishing nets he spoke of. He saw through my shyness and saw, perhaps, the true extent of my hunger, which had nothing to do with food. I sing of the London streets where I wandered each day, Soho, Piccadilly, Camden Town; I sing of the 50p tiny, orange notebooks that became the chronicle of my inner life, my real life, which I carried with me everywhere and which read, now, like wonder shaped by the hands of someone too in love with everything to see anything clearly; I sing of a gift so precious it haunts me like a dream, a dream that fell into my lap, the dream to travel and to wander and to not want for anything except the impressions of this wandering; of the West End and its pubs and theaters and street musicians in Covent Garden, the Jimi Hendrix look-alike who is probably still there; of the British Museum and the rich, mellow scent of roasted peanuts near its iron gates; I sing of nights in the flat alone, sitting on the ledge of my bedroom, which overlooked a small court-yard, and beyond it, the passing lights of trains, whose passengers are still with me in their brief, serious faces; of smoking cigarettes for the first time and listening to Chet Baker with one leg dangling out the window. I sing of all of this and hope someday I can thank her who made it possible, the woman in the institution, the woman with money who didn't know what to do with it, so she gave it away to people who had not yet been born.

Recitative

During *Faust* I looked around to see if others were as shell-shocked as I, to see if their lives were similarly uprooted and tossed into the air.

I couldn't read their dark faces. I couldn't measure my own surprise compared with the countenances of others. I remember I suddenly just wanted to reach out and hold someone's hand, anyone's hand, to solidify by touch the electricity of the moment. But it was enough to be in the darkened theater, to be here as a witness to the beginning of my real life, which no one else could truly witness anyway. I didn't want to be anywhere else. And the intensity of my own emotions surprised, chastened me; I didn't want anyone (and yet I did) to be with me.

Maybe all musical moments—when we are suddenly transported out of ourselves or more deeply into ourselves—are case studies in fate, a collision course between who we are and what we will become. Maybe we can't divide the music from ourselves, or even from the turnstiles of history. Maybe music and only music nails the conversion of the innocent into a world of astonishment and grandeur, each note and plucked string and dying tremolo a remnant of the heart straining at the end of its leash.

I want to love almost unconsciously, almost instinctively. I wish I could let this love come from me less from effort and meditation, and more like a fountain, not turned on by my own hand. It seems to me, when you have to love any other way, you are weighing and discriminating. —journal entry, London, 1990

One night I went to see a concert at the Royal Festival Hall: Tchaikovsky's First Piano Concerto. I sat in the back and watched the patrons stream in and take their seats. I thought they were so dainty then, so frail: I remember most of the audience as dignified, older people, old women with necklaces at their throats and distinguished gentlemen with clipped or careless mustaches. I remember them as though they came through an immense fog, insubstantial then distinct in the bright lights of the auditorium and memory. I remember the old people best, coming again for music at the twilight of their lives as I was just beginning mine. To put down their ten- or twenty-pound notes for these seats seemed suddenly such a strange, dear price to pay: to listen to music just this side of the Thames was a small miracle I still can't get over. I watched them take their seats, fascinated, perfect strangers folding their overcoats into discrete bundles as if they had done this a hundred times and knew the simple ritual some place in their aging bones. I saw them talk to each other and smile, or stare out vacantly over the rows. One woman smiled to me as if over an ocean of time, her white hair shining in a bun of dizzying beauty, then turned away again to resume her seat.

I sat in the row behind her, dressed like a backpacker. I was nervous. I wrapped my program into a kind of cylinder, and my hands were clammy. I was nervous to be there, my second home, the Royal Festival Hall; I was nervous, perhaps because I had had too much coffee. Or perhaps because my days in London were winding down, and after this I would soon be going home. I was nervous because suddenly the stakes of music had gotten very high; I went to it with improbable hopes and expectations, not so much for the quality of the sound but the evocations it might release in me. I wanted to share this nervousness with someone, but I was alone. Suddenly it was no good being alone: where before I had deliberately gone to these events by myself out of a kind of near-defiance (because I thought, foolishly, no one would want to at that age), suddenly I wanted to share the music with someone else. I had fantasies about this secret other, the one who would take this same music and go to other places with me. Man or woman, it didn't matter. Just to sit next to this other and feel the music would be more than enough. Suddenly music had taken on the contours of travel, but I was not going anywhere; suddenly, inexplicably, the stakes were of an entirely different order. I knew then that I was in trouble, though of a strange and beguiling kind; I knew then that music that is not shared is of the most heartbreaking variety—and that most music cannot be shared, especially that which goes to the very roots of ourselves. I was fooling myself in this daydream of this "other." There could be no other because all of what had led me here— wandering in London day after day, ducking into this or that cafe, not even noticing the street or name of the cafe, in fact my whole interior life, which was this same heedless wandering inside my skull far away back home—was wrapped up inviolate in my blood like a secret package or pang that only music could release. I did not yet have a name for or means of expressing this sleepwalking anyway. It was just there in the blood all along, waiting patiently for the day when it might have a name and spring all by itself into being, which I think now is always a tragic moment. I was nervous because a part of me realized someday I would die, with all the riches of my secret life trapped inside. The pianist launched into the Tchaikovsky, his sandy, long hair flashing under the bright lights of the stage like stalks of iridescent corn. I watched him as if hypnotized from a great distance—and that same distance seems shorter now, and farther.

After the concert I walked over the bridge from Royal Festival Hall to the Embankment Tube. A homeless man with flecks of bread in his beard played his wooden leg like a banjo and smiled. The air was damp and cold, the stars polished and bright. The Thames ran like mystery under my feet. I stared at it a long time, now turning into then, and the river pulled itself back under the bridge like a dark cape holding the secrets of everyone who had ever stood there, the secrets of music and death.

Bugs of Noise

What I mean is possibly this, that the noises of the world, so various in themselves and which I used to be so clever at distinguishing from one another, had been dinning at me for so long, always the same old noises, as gradually to have merged into a single noise, so that all I heard was one vast continuous buzzing. —Samuel Beckett, *Malone Dies*

I THINK THAT SOMEWHERE in my ears is a tiny suggestible bug, small and delicate with the lightness of tissue paper, that acts as the amplifier of all artificial sound, so that I dread the sounds of sirens, traffic, bad mufflers, people talking outside; scrapes of chairs in the apartment above, blow driers, loud obnoxious voices; pens dropped on wooden floors, small dogs barking their sopranos, the blare of a television or commercial radio; or any noise I can't somehow control or diminish. I have been weakened by this parasite over time until I can no longer resort to reason or kindness when it comes to any noise that does not agree with me. My only recourse is to shut off the source of the noise or to get away from it, or to stuff cotton—anything soft— into my ears as a buffer between the noise and my precious, sensitive bug, which I imagine is lettuce green and translucent, only changing color to a strobe-like red when it is hearing something that violates its peace and comfort. The bug dreads any noise it deems offensive, and its small body vibrates back and forth in furious agitation, centering it like a small pulley that brings the noise closer and closer until all I can do is focus all my conscious energy upon it. Sometimes this sound appears in a synesthesia of dread, a blotch of malevolent purple or slash of urine yellow in my mind's eye, or a drooping hollow in my stomach of things to come (new loud neighbors), or even the quick snatch of anger burning at the plates of my skull; and the more the bug vibrates, the more desperate I become to put distance between myself and the noise. No doubt this is a strange and troubling malady, but like any host I have learned to live with my bug, and it has learned to live with me. In symbiosis we have an understanding: my bug starts jiggling when noise is around, punching the sides of my brain like a troubled inmate, and I take the necessary measures to buffer the noise or to get away from it. These are the only two possible solutions — everything else is an unbearable compromise. Even the telephone ringing is an intrusion upon its well-laid nest, which I think is nestled somewhere between the two hemispheres of my brain, like a snug and warm fingertip in the downward crease. There the bug wants only to not be disturbed, and I respect its warm nook and haven because it is a part of me.

Because sometimes I think everyone in an eighty-foot radius can hear me because I can hear them: their sounds arrive from every conceivable angle and purpose, from pedestrians walking by talking about the weather and to their dogs, to my old next-door neighbor turning on her tap water and rinsing dishes. We are awash in fields and particles of sound.

One afternoon when I was coming home from the store, I paused in the hallway at my front door. Across the way I could hear my neighbor Caroline pleading, crying, weeping on the telephone. I stood for a moment listening. She was asking her boyfriend not to hang up, not to go; she kept repeating "No, Brent, no" in woeful, continuous pleas that rose and quavered with each syllable, rising and falling in hurt and desolation. I heard her voice like a revelation. She was facing the prospect of loneliness, and I was listening to the final break. Normally so cheerful and bouncy almost to the point of embarrassment (she often leaves little treats at my door, a movie or a batch of brownies, always accompanied by a cheery, clear note followed with a !), she was now her one and true self, a voice crying out not to be left behind, not to be discarded. She was an island of sobs. Yet I continued to listen. The hurt was so real and palpable I almost wanted to knock on her door. I hated Brent. But weren't these sounds meant to be her own? Couldn't she fall apart in the privacy of her own home without anyone hearing?

Weren't some sounds meant to be private? Such a strange admixture of guilt, embarrassment, and real concern came over me; I didn't know if this was my cue to reach out and console her. I didn't know what to do. I stood there for another moment, flummoxed, and then fumbled for my key. Her sobs filled the vacant hallway behind me and I closed the door.

Sometimes the desire for quiet is so great that I arrange my whole day surreptitiously around it—like a secret vice. I sit in the quiet apartment and absorb the silence. The walls are my friends. I rely on the absence of people and movement. I have stopped questioning the nature and source of my peculiar affliction; I respect my bug's space and it respects mine. Together we have an unspoken agreement (of course) not to falsely disturb each other's equilibrium; if I could, I would feed the bug breadcrumbs or crackers, whatever it wanted, if only I had the dexterity and means to safely reach into my head. In lieu of that, I just try to keep it happy. The bug has evolved in the corridor between my thoughts. I imagine even now the bug is safely ensconced in the slippery, living matter of my brain, not feeding off it exactly, only finding refuge from the impossibly noisy modern day world. And it is noisy. The bug is gentle on this point, understanding: it knows somehow that sounds are also necessary, vital not only to its living host but to the equilibrium of the universe. It is noise, ceaseless, abrupt, or sustained, that violates the bug's glowing translucent shell like rays from some unholy sun, noise that can disrupt the very process of its life and render it a dot of trembling jelly that sends tremors through my head, like a tiny electromagnetic quake. And it is noise—mark my words—that will undo the clarity of moral vision in our time and those to come, noise that will reduce the potential harmony of human beings with each other and themselves to meaningless incoherent babble.

The bug does not mind birds singing in the early morning, actually likes the soughing of wind through trees, Bach and Beethoven (sometimes even loud), rain storms and even thunder. But it detests lawn mowers and motorcycles. Cement trucks and helicopters feed its frenzy. It flips upside down when someone's car alarm goes off. Even the innocuous sounds of people slamming their front doors is enough to jar the bug from its cozy nest and lend to it a frantic throbbing. I like to think of my bug as a gentle little soul who favors the tranquil sounds of water rushing in a mountain stream, the ring of someone's laughter (but not too loud), or a cardinal singing its heart out on a branch. Anything but the harsh, grating noises of metal on metal, jet airplanes, the throbbing bass of someone's stereo, or a speed boat. The bug in essence is telling me (or whispering): "We're two of a kind, you and me; let's get through this together; but if you disregard my wishes, I'll make your life a living hell." Thus the world in all its multifarious sounds is severely divided into two kinds: good ones and bad ones (noise). There is no middle ground. We live among competing pools of sound. Even the sound of my own voice can be a bad sound if it rises above a certain level. Then the bug is doubly irate, clicking its many heels in frenzied hurry, kicking at my brain. Shut up. Just shut up. It respects human voices only as far as timbre and volume. It admires sweet curses murmured in a whisper and deplores loud whoops from young men in pickup trucks. It likes conversation of all kinds and hates ceaseless chatter. Babble is like putting a Walkman on its head. My bug's predilections are quite impossible: it doesn't understand the need to speak loudly, except perhaps to a group of volunteer firemen who must put out a raging barbecue pit. It doesn't abide any noise. Even as I write this, an old, rusty Buick wobbles by on squeaky axles, scissoring back and forth with the labor of grazing metal, like the quickened heartbeat of some infernal machine, and my bug digs down stubbornly, chewing at a brainy wall to mark its dissatisfaction and rage.

Once in my old apartment a neighbor above woke me in the middle of the night with his heavy, plodding feet: they sounded like snowshoes weighted down with lead clasps. Because the apartment building had wooden floors, and because this neighbor in particular had been responsible for countless noises before, the bug inside my head began its strange paranoid dance, began to tremble back and forth, gnaw at my head, whimper its soundless wail, so I had no choice but to get up and try to understand—to see—the source of my bug's panic. I got up out of bed, dressed hastily, cursing my neighbor unmercifully, and circled the building at 3:00 A.M. I wanted to see from outside if he was really awake, if my bug and I truly had to endure his clumsiness for yet another night. And as I stood on the sidewalk in the snow, dressed haphazardly like a woebegone traveler far from home, a clear glow emanated from his bedroom window, and I saw his bald head and wire-rimmed glasses bobbing back and forth. It was awful. It was the sinking feeling of complete despair: I could not imagine the hell of his footsteps night after night or his loud booming voice that terrorized the delicate bug in my brain; it was no good, we couldn't live in the same staggered place in harmony. When noise is above me, I dread it like an oncoming illness. It comes from nowhere like a stampede of horses. In its sudden volume and fury it takes on the qualities of a personal assault, an affront against one's domestic universe, a violation and a mockery. It is hell setting up shop. Such noises seem directly aimed at one's sense of mental balance and peace. They rocket out from their sources like cannonballs, or insinuate themselves with the long trail of toxic repetition: some noises, like overhearing drunk conversations in the middle of the night, make one despair even of the whole human race, of how we have come to be so crude and sluggish, so foul-mouthed, so *stupid*. I cannot escape these prejudices, even as I write them, prejudices my bug feeds on. We were not meant to bellow in the middle of the night, or drive around in jalopies with fenders dragging on the ground. We were not designed for five-foot woofers in our bedrooms. I reject our modern noises. I refute them.

But standing in the snow, watching my neighbor, knowing his very footsteps were like stabs from a voodoo curse, I began to wonder about my sanity. His voice was a bowling ball flying down an alley in the gutter, and his steps—his huge, careless, flopping steps—were the measure of a persecution and affront to my ears, the quality and intensity of which I have never experienced before or since I have moved to a quieter place.

The burden of a sensitivity is a special cause: fair skin is a bull's eye for the sun; shellfish is an invitation for hives to run like an army over one's neck and shoulders; bee stings can be fatal; cat dander causes sneezing fits; the sight of blood makes one fall away in a dead faint.

Our sensitivities are everywhere and hidden, protected in a closet from too much exposure. My bug is no different.

The bug is short and squat, no bigger than a grain of rice, with a clear green shell that is polished like a fiberglass dome; its eyes are invisible, and its antennae are graceful twigs that hang languidly like two overgrown eyebrows. It has approximately two thousand feet, which move in waves when it is climbing. It is your run-of-the-mill bug, unexceptional except in agitation. If it were human, it might resemble a composite junior high math teacher who has settled into the same sedentary lifestyle over the course of twenty years: egg sandwich for lunch, a flip through the sports section, a chronic brushing of the nose with thumb and forefinger. A routine that does not vary. But when aroused my bug's fury is legion, emanating through every part of its body until it trembles as if on fire, its whole body a glowing red and ready to burst like a high-pressured artery. My bug is set in its ways, intractable, infantile, woefully inadequate before the noises of the world. And it never appreciates irony or any other finer use of noise, like sitcom boings and studio audiences. It eschews cheap laughs. Madness is not even in its repertoire. It does not move until something violates its peace and quiet, and then it scurries up to pull and punch, tear and rage, like the id gone wild. There is no dialogue between us. I say and do everything for it, and it does not know gratitude. It is like an entrenched tenant who pays his rent, keeps his doors closed, and periodically goes bonkers by kicking the door off its hinges. So it cringes at jackhammers, spins its head like a top at leaf blowers, winces at garbage trucks, and goes ballistic at sirens. When I try to say, Listen: someone could be seriously hurt or even dying in that ambulance, it shakes its head in a blur until it almost creates its own buzzing. It kicks when it can't sleep and does somersaults at souped-up Chevies. It likes children but hates schoolbuses; it doesn't mind Ferris wheels but shudders at roller coasters; it likes the sound of coffee perking but loathes grinders; it likes swings but detests merry-go-rounds. The list is encyclopedic, infinite. For every like there is a dislike, for every sound an immediate reaction. The bug lives only to react to noise.

I sometimes wonder if the bug wants me to go deaf, to slam just enough of itself into me to damage the inner ear. But I don't think so.

It realizes that I need music, that certain sounds are food, and that the proper place of silence is to restore my appreciation for real sounds, the sounds that matter. Voices in rooms, long distance phone calls, concerts, children playing, robins, the chatter of squirrels, thunder and wind, trees thrashing, waves, long grass, old records, murmurs and tinkling of silverware in an old cafe, the scraping of a broom, the groans of lovemaking. These are good and necessary sounds, if not wholesome. They give expression to the hunger and music of our lives—and my bug is still then, snug and satisfied. It does not tremble or vibrate anymore. My bug lives on in the Saran Wrap of my brain, burrowing down into its nook until it sits there in its unappeasable lodging. I think we all have these bugs to one degree or another, and they need to be acknowledged for what they are: the vanguards against noise, those chariots of meaninglessness. These bugs are tiny, lurking seeds that make us confront sound in the hit and run of chaos. Today I celebrate my parasite, whose whole body pulls on the fibers of my aural awareness; with each pluck I reconfigure my concept of sound and go like a sleepwalker toward those that communicate something mysterious or essential. The other sounds—noise—my bug rails at, and I go where it asks me, shutting the window or door with a shudder. In this way my whole world is shrinking, as my bug inches deeper into the gray matter of my brain as a cushion against the inarticulate rush of modern noise.

Empty Cages

PAY SECRET ATTENTION to abandoned shopping carts, those derelicts of renegade shopping sprees taken from their native stores, upended Humpty-Dumpty-style over the backs of fences, into bushes, near Dumpsters and rotting mattresses, some of them stuffed full of moldy bread, broken belts, car batteries, diapers. They will never go that way again, where thoughtful hands inspect ripe fruit, feeling for bruises; where the impulse buy becomes a heart-thumping necessity, the pause and ponder of small yearnings. They will never again carry the needs of the elderly or poor, or fit neatly into rows of their collapsible brethren. All of that is over. Who knew they would end up at the bottom of a gulch, tied to a hubcap in the rain? What midnight need or disrepair brought them to the edge of oblivion and then pushed them over into the spontaneous junkyard blooming like steely vines in alleys and ditches? Why here, now, strewn about broken-down neighborhoods where towels are used for curtains, and windows have the vacant, half-shuttered look of swollen black eyes? I've seen them on my walks for years, more and more of them roaming away from stores, as if the homelessness of shopping carts has become a national epidemic, a secret hurt. And what if I decided to make one of these carts my own, to push it all the way home into my living room, my bedroom, the spare room I call an office? I can hear the rumble of the poor wheels not made for concrete sidewalks or long hauls, and the looks of passersby who might think, There goes another one who didn't quite make it. I could put so much into one of these carts, all of my shoes and records, a healthy dose of apples, and move out across the country, one or two miles-per-hour, the steady drone of stony wheels becoming a fine white noise around me.

I see them all over, homeless people, pushing these carts past urban ruins, wandering in rain and sunshine up and down the streets, with their balls of hairy twine and all manner of cans, bottles, and tarps. They make these carts their moving caravan, and if I see their lips moving silently, maybe it's because they are talking to someone none of us can see; maybe they are holding counsel with people who can't touch them anymore. This, too, is a kind of temptation; I've been disconnected for decades, not quite fitting in, not quite useful. The gleaming cage could hold everything I would ever need, and it would still be too much. Then the carts become something else, the moving wonder of damaged lives, the unpretentious and quiet declaration that unlike 99 percent of us, here what you see is what you get. These are not prettified ventures; they are the one movement or faith in everything they will ever have, and this is something to learn from and to consider. No garages, no computers, no hair gel or workout videos, no miracle of new clothes or coffee makers. No comforters, curling irons, prints of Monet, cucumber slicers, tax records from two years ago, ironing boards, fat dictionaries. Just caged necessity under the sky and the threat of letting it roll away from you once and for all.

II

I wonder how it got there, that cart hanging upside down: I wonder how it made it up the six-foot fence to hang precariously, willy-nilly. What were the sequence and the steps, the reasons and the method? And who will disengage it now? Each time I wander by this cart, I wonder anew at the strange ingenuity of desperation. This could make you laugh or make you cry, or make you cry while laughing. I know then that my own failures are not very far behind. For some reason the shopping cart brings this home to me. The shopping cart is an emblem of failure and the originality of failure, failure that's been pushed to the margins of every city lot.

Here it is suspended five feet above the ground, overlooking a fenced-off area where no one ever goes, egg cartons and trash bags pile up like hoodlums come home to die. Some mornings you can pause here overlooking this ugliness (if you'd want to). You imagine the empty bottles of brandy and see the drunken man wrestling with freakish strength the cart into place, beating the odds by rolling it up *the fence*, monkeying and cursing the damn thing the whole goddamn way, getting it to a point where it's almost there, just the edge of it now, tippy-toe, off-balance, rollers spinning aimlessly, still hanging where it can fall back on his head, sweating, cursing, one more push, one more inch, flakes of corn chips in his beard, then the sudden clicking into place for all time. No one will ever use this cart again. No one will surpass this act of originality and rage, no poet, no rapper: this upended shopping cart is a symbol of bitter, unrighteous times, a contempt for consumer goods so deep it borders on the pathological. It hangs there because it has to, because maybe the drunk man will never get what he wants in this life, he's pissed off, raging, past caring that night, past tenderness, past mercy. Try to get this shopping cart off the fence.

III

You see them everywhere, pushing these carts to God knows where, the basket full of throwaways, cans, bottles, and sleeping bags, lotion, flashlights, jugs, stacked newspapers. They push them and stare straight ahead, a kind of tunnel vision, and you hear them before you see them, rumbling down your street like the lone, dry call of a hollow bird, careening here because they have to, pushing ahead in a neighborhood that does not want them. Wild-eyed or tame, with greasy shirts and hair, they are invading your neighborhood one by one, people as alien as creatures from outer space. And what is it they are collecting but what we throw away? Why are they picking up after us after all this time? Who knew? And this is the real world, you suddenly think, this is the world I've been avoiding all of my life: homeless, raging human beings whose dreams and patterns of thinking would astonish you. They take these shopping carts from places you go to buy fruit and soap, where the aisles are clean and polished, where the floors gleam like birthday candles. And they take these carts away, number 561 or 7, out into the sun and rain, cramming them full with their whole itinerant lives, in ways never conceived of by the manufacturers. They take these carts and set up camp in the invisible city, the makeshift tents and lean-tos, in alleys, backyards. They hang these carts upside down on fences, roll them into cars, take them back, pogoing over bumps and cracks, fill them up with the soft husks of corn, abandon them, leave them to rust. They're using what is set out before them, a small, gleaming fortress on roller skates, and the sound they make is the slow drone of the woebegone, the music of fools, visionaries, seers.

Here comes a pair pushing one up a steep hill, shoelaces moping, mouths drooling, the cart full of broken, dusty fans, one with a T-shirt stained piss-yellow from sweat or smoking, the other a skinny, bald old man who can't stop shaking. They are pushing up the hill in a slow-moving curse, as if the baggage of their entire lives is a burden that leaves them climbing here, climbing forever. The small fans won't keep them cool on this hot September day. They are pushing, saying things to each other in whispers, cackles. I give them a wide berth when I see them; I move to the other side of the street. I give them everything, my secret haunts and wishes, my deepest fears, my whole heart. They are moving up the hill and disappearing into the sun, the cart gleaming like tinfoil or knives, fans like pinwheels of the vast and heartbreaking usefulness of what we throw out and what we leave behind.

Las Vegas in Three Parts

I

FIRST I NOTICED how almost everyone on the sidewalk carried his or her own water in a plastic bottle that sparkled in the sun. This brief necklace of light could startle or astonish you momentarily, if only to see the city anew; it was just like an aureole that sang about the sun in delicate bars above hearing, one of the few things Las Vegas could offer that was genuine and clear. You soon learn that carrying water in this city is sacred, indeed the only sacred, inviolable thing in this place that combines every religion and pursuit of mammon in one precious stream. Even gambling is not possible without it: water is the root that makes this city real and makes it false, underwriting each activity like a ghost rider appearing out of the desert. I looked for this rider every day in subtle places, watching to see how it made this desert city come together. I was never disappointed. Even the geckos knew the gig was up when clouds appeared; they flicked their tongues upward to anticipate the drops that rarely came.

I remember the man with the shaved head and his sparkling water bottle easing down West Sahara, and I suddenly knew each of us was staying there on the desert's own terms, which were always the terms of water. The stark clarity of this point came home to me every day. Then the city threw off its dancer's robes and fancy red lipstick and became just itself, a naked and leggy gal doing her thing in a town far away from home. This was the moment I fell most in love with it and rushed to embrace its absurdities and the desperation of its waste. For Vegas is ridiculous and sublime by turns: nowhere in any pocket of it is it not burning down to the last cigarette or poker chip, inviting awe in the radiance of the sun. I grew curious about the force of water in a place where it was scarce, less than four inches a year. My parents retired there a few years ago. So visiting them, I came to realize, would always be a reckoning with water; after all, maybe singing about the sun in an aureole of light is not such a bad way to live. Because Las Vegas exists on time stolen from the desert, someday it will have to pay for its prodigal ways: stone must return to stone, even the artificial stone of Ceasar's and Bellagio.

The desert and its threadbare ways are always creeping up on the city proper, sprouting here and there in vacant lots to reveal its true essence. Wherever the city is not artificially green or maintained, the scrabbled earth comes in like an underlying grid of dread, working its way toward the oblivion of synthetic things. You can feel it beneath your feet if you're very still and quiet, like the dead turning slightly in their graves. You see it in half-finished golf courses, you see it off the freeway, creeping beyond the other side of the median. You see it in the Stratosphere downtown, as it wobbles as if it were a scepter on fire, trembling before your eyes in the common rubble of infernal waves; how can it stand up to this sun day after day? What keeps it from toppling into ruin? I began to look for other, shining things untouched by singing water, things that glittered by themselves. I was soon disappointed to find only the usual suspects: chrome fenders, the jewelry of older and younger inhabitants alike—all a piece of blindness—windows and mirrors of office buildings and casinos, the racing neon of marquees shooting strobes past each other in the circuitry of their wires.

Did I expect to be blinded, to be led away from my impressions toward a new understanding? Did I want something in the city to redeem it, to make me love the glitz and two-way mirrors that contained the cynicism of fun?

You could study the rock beds leading to McCarran Airport; you could count each one of them as a loaf fresh from the latitudes of hell; but none of them would explain the need for water and glittering things in a place woeful to both. Later, toward the end of one of my stays, I realized nothing indigenous gleamed here because that would only magnify the power of the sun, a god incommensurate with human frivolity. So I stayed with the shaved man's singing water bottle for reasons I still don't know.

Every time I fly out to Las Vegas I make a secret promise to myself to try to discover part of the true nature of this place; maybe this is a starting point. Maybe it is the only real point to Las Vegas there is.

II

Then I went to Red Rock Canyon, just west of the city, feeling a strange kind of pull, like any seeking pilgrim. I went as if it had been calling me all of my life, which of course it had. The day was unseasonably hot, even for that parched and desolate region: 108 degrees by 11:00 A.M., so I had the trails to myself. It could have been two centuries ago, or ten.

The only sound I heard was the whine of an insect whose hollow voice sounded like a narrow, glass tube the circumference of a willow reed. It came from the edge of a cliff off the Calico Trunks Trail to inquire about eternity; I tipped my head back under my floppy hat and listened. It came from so far away it was like a lost thread looking for its spool, or a filament of hair that buzzed with the vast emptiness around it, so charged with the stuff of silence it overflowed into this tiny, mote-like source. I was lucky to be among those rocks, standing still and listening. Maybe it found a home in some damp, unseen place that was shrinking to the size of a button. But I will never forget this sound, a sustained whine slightly above the register of complaint. Is the desert a comic place? I didn't think so then and I do not now.

I knew the water I carried at my side was pretty much all I would ever have. This knowledge grew in force every twenty feet as I made my way on the rocky footpath laid out before me. My bottle sang in the sun, too, but I did my best to preserve its shining aureole for my eyes only, to keep the water cool as long as I could. I thought then I could be happy wandering around those rocks for a few years, but maybe I was fooling myself. I left Las Vegas behind to hike here alone. It was like looking for a lost silver spoon in the desert; it was like finding myself lucid after a Fata Morgana went away.

I saw a clipped edge of the sky cleanly halved by the rock faces above, a movement in stone so fine and ancient it was like a wave captured in time, only here, of course, nothing remained forever how it was. It was moving, even as I thought, toward a new horizon. The sky kept pulling its blue veil around the cosmos, with only a shred of cloud here and there to give its passage a fleeting reference point. Looking up this way at the sky, with the rock ledges one hundred or two hundred feet above, was the cleanest feeling I have ever known. I felt awe in that place, as it ushered in a new awareness devoid of personal pronouns; the desert is no place for the ego.

The senses are heightened because they are poised on the rim of eternity; everything is a kind of seeing and listening, as if these are the only ways to bore through falseness. The scrub brush and the Joshua trees made a go of it because they could. I thought then if I could get to the heart of the Joshua's secret I might call mine a worthy life; I might call it blessed beyond its capacity to endure joy. But I was not put to the test. They dot the landscape like hair-shirted monks who are past withering. One Joshua tree, a bushy-legged and furry fellow the height of a small refrigerator, stood slightly crooked in the sun, standing on one leg. He held his crooked limbs like some strange posture inviting ridicule or rain; I noted the long patience of his stand, the dignity of his dread. Someday I would show such dignity in the face of withering heat, or that same heat would exact from me this same kind of devotion. How do we know trees do not have souls? I saw them standing there as surely as that place got hotter and hotter, making sand under my heels.

At the end of the trail I was rewarded for my journey. A small pool, much diminished, formed a kind of oasis surrounded by a box canyon of red and yellow stone. I lay many minutes under the eaves of an outcropping on a clean, long tablet leading to the lip of the pond. It sloped slightly, maybe five degrees, and I closed my eyes and thought of earlier times. Every once in a while a bird flew by or chirped, and I could hear the breeze in the long weeds. The sum of a life is just so many moments, and nothing more. As I lay in the canyon I thought at least this one day I had done something clean and pure; it was no small victory for me. A scorpion could crawl up behind me and give me a fatal sting; the stones above could shift and fall, crushing my skull; I could have lost my water and bumped my head, waking long after nightfall, shivering and incoherent; but none of these would mitigate the strange beauty of this place or my alien presence in it. I thought without prejudice or remorse how strange that my skin was white, or that Las Vegas should lie so many miles to the southeast; all of the hullabaloo of that infamous place seemed much exaggerated and of no use here. Just stone, scrub, and this precious water small creatures came to drink. Before I drifted off to sleep the wind came up suddenly over the ridge and gave the tank a harmless thrashing. Time had no purchase here, no place to set its small teeth to chattering. I rested and felt restored on that hard bed, dreaming of water, and how it made the long, strange journey to the end of my feet; then we were just two pools, holding on to our aqueous blues and greens, landing here by coincidence in the middle of the desert.

III

There were only windows looking out to the same horizons, the desert pulling the eye in every direction, a panorama of distance. Each window I looked out of confirmed my doubts about Las Vegas as a permanent abode; we were surrounded by mountains and sheer distance at the bottom of a bowl, no doubt about it. I pulled into a 7-11 off Sahara to buy a phone card. Everyone who came seemed preternaturally tan and smoking a cigarette, and one cadaverous gentleman was playing video poker in the corner. I studied him surreptitiously for awhile. The slow way his hands moved suggested he had been there for quite some time, maybe his entire adult life. A clean blue shirt was pressed to his rail-thin body, and his blond ducktail was feathered like a bush that had been raked by solar winds. Dark pouches sagged under his eyes, the only place on his whole person that carried excess skin. I sincerely hope he was winning. But his movements were so automatic as to suggest a slow, chronic leak of funds, or the smallest accretion of quarters, which amounts almost to the same thing. What would startle him out of his chair? What would jump-start for him a whole new way of life? People filed in and out of the small store, dressed for the heat, many of them tattooed and beleaguered. There was no real view in the 7-11, and this in retrospect I took as some kind of sign; hunkered in his corner, playing his poker with an illuminated screen that cast a faint green glow on his sun-darkened face, I wondered what brought him to this place, why he sought forgetfulness in a 7-11 a few miles from the strip. Something vital was slipping away.

His simple playing evoked a catastrophe of waste that temporarily floored me; I tried to understand the import of this brief encounter with a man who didn't know I was watching him, didn't know I saw the dirt under his fingernails or his Pall Malls. Maybe to some this is a version of heaven, a democratic dream, that a man or woman could gamble for hours in a gas station as people came and went. I don't know. But surely somewhere else there was a discord fomenting in Las Vegas that was even then setting up a reckoning, not out of pique or spite, but something emerging from the desert itself; I could feel it biding its time, leaning in. Looking out of any window or from even atop the Voodoo Lounge at the Rio, something lay in wait beyond all of us. I thought then each window in Vegas provided a glimpse of a necessary doom that was as beautiful as it was mysterious, as far-reaching as it was untouchable. The singing water bottle would not let me go. The stones at Red Rock burned with immutable fire, and my ducktailed friend will play his hand well into the grave. These are the only facts about Las Vegas that continue to haunt me. From them I learned that the desert lay revealed in every direction, and that there was no other reality.

Driving to the River

To know is to be alien to rivers. — Richard Hugo

D RIVING TO THE RIVER is listening to the highway moan in cold asphalt, syllables that rasp a clean wave from Omaha to Lincoln. Driving to the river is looking ahead, past the curve of Interstate 80 where the horizon glows in soft ambers at sunrise and the sudden, gleaming promise of the Platte River near Ashland. Driving to the river is finding that delicate bird bone in the schoolyard you could almost put in your mouth, a bone that has waited months and years for your small hand to bring it back to the land of the living and the dying. It is the primordial yearning of all living things that sings in the blood, vowelless and clear, past humming and breathing, taking us forward, taking us back.

I make the commute between Omaha and Lincoln three days a week, sometimes four — fifty miles across plains quilted between rolling hills and farm land. I hit the Platte driving west, and sometimes it breaks into view like a revelation of poured honey, or the sheen of a knife-edge that would cut straight to your heart; then something in me grows still and very quiet, until the water as I drive over it counts off the seconds of my life in slow river time. I turn my attention again to the road, the sky, renewed and somewhat chastened. Rivers do this to me. They are a way to measure time, to ask yourself what you're doing with your life, and for whom. Over the years it has become a ritual, a trip into the meaning of water itself. When I reach the river and cross over, something crosses over in me too: maybe it's the sheer presence of water, the dynamism of the living force. Sometimes I don't want to keep going, but I do. I want to stay near it, to see its muddy banks and cargo of branches.

In Nebraska, water has a special status, the stamp of the divine. You don't see it loose and grand very often except in floods and rivers. You must imagine it, conjure it in your head as the one element held back for special occasions. It's not an everyday occurrence. Because of this, driving across the river—any river—is like a brief fling with heaven, over almost before you know it. I come down between hills and valleys, I lose the NPR station between Gretna and Ashland, and it's just the whining road underneath the tires. Semis fly by, hauling their rigs behind them, red taillights glowing like wet cherries in the dawn.

Once in a while trucks pass me carrying cattle to market. I see their sides bulging out with frayed hairs in the serrated holes—holes that taper out so as not, I think, to cut into their skin prematurely—their tired, mangy hair and the occasional shock of an eyeball white and glassy from staring too long. I follow those eyeballs down the highway. They are the color of their own homogenized milk or porcelain, as big as a baby's fist; they never blink in the fleeting dawn, going past. They never see me looking after them, never see much of anything at all. I follow them into the darkness. Sometimes I smell them, too, the stench of fear, shit, and death. They are being hauled to slaughter as we approach the river: four miles, three miles, two miles, one. I see a tail that looks like it has been electrocuted, frayed wires of a broom good for nothing. Do they know where they are going? Do they know what it means to be transported in a rocking cage of death? Do I? The stench carries for a mile, but then the truck and its precious haul fade again and the hills come back, lighter than before. They reach the river before me, before I figure out what it means: the cars, the darkness, the emerging dawn and the river at the bottom of it, the river we come to whether we want to or not, the river we must cross to get to the other side, people, cattle, and babies buckled into car seats, driving to the river.

Sometimes driving is a passage into ourselves where we do not know the destination. And the river is beyond us, waiting as it has always been. Some mornings I watch the faces going by: they are speeding forward, staring past the horizon into what only they can see. Some are sipping coffee, some are talking on the phone, some are brushing their hair at seventy m.p.h. I wait for the highway to hold them. I wait for it to hold me. I watch the road until I'm absorbed into its great winding hypnosis, until I can't escape it myself. Then I wait for the river. I wait for it like the summation of my life, the earth leveling out; I wait for it to strengthen me. More and more I wait for this when I drive to the river, but only recently have I become aware of it. So I cross it and feel a brief catch of hope in my heart, like thousands of others each day. I cross it and feel that this driving is a kind of prayer, one that produces the necessary feelings of awe. I pay homage to the river because I cannot help it; it lies in its misty shroud like a beautiful, naked woman disappearing into a shawl.

Does that make me a pilgrim in the growing light, even if I am just going between two midwestern cities? Does this prove the conjunction of water, sky, and soulfulness forever and ever? Am I ever exempt from the mystery of water? Is anyone? Do I deserve this water, this moment, this sudden balm of peacefulness that takes me over the river? The answer is no, but I take it anyway: I take everything I can get, the tiredness, the coffee, the search for deer at the water's edge, and the shifting sand bars that will not stay in place. They will not stay in place. They move like patches of new earth in a shifting garden, until — surprise! — there they are: oases of sandy retreat in a skein of water. I watch for these sandbars, count them off like old friends. It's strange to see them move and disappear, taking on new shapes near the banks and eddies. I see and wait for all of this in a few seconds, seconds I will carry to my grave. Driving to the river is like this sometimes. I've learned to love it flying by at seventy-five m.p.h. I ask it to give me things, to give me hope and reasons to keep going, to give me the penny dread of destination, the meaning of traveled miles. I've come too many mornings not to notice something, finally. But all I've really noticed is the humility of my small passage in the dark. I wait for the river. I will always wait for the river. It has become the meridian of my day, the meridian of my life. I think the sight of the Platte is a blessing for me, though I don't know why. It lasts only a few short seconds. I have counted them, and they add up only to a day, a month, a year, a whole life driving between two cities, driving again to the river.

* * *

Now the Platte disappears into a thin mist, the curve of its body fading like the edge of that woman whose body goes on forever. I can't see where it bends. You couldn't contain the spirit of this river in any painting or symphony, any poem. It's too deep down for symbols, or the colors of a palette. I look to the east this morning. There over the rim of the earth a small profusion of pastels grows lighter in the sky, taking on shape and brightness. I ask the river to give me a mouth to say this sky, to sing it if I can; but I know I can only mouth the praise in words as dry as sticks. The banks fly by smudge-like, ghostly. There is no sun yet. For a few, brief seconds I memorize the mood of the river, which is waiting only to become itself. I know I will be back, and then the mist will be gone, and the river will be sharp and bright again, a razor on its side. Maybe then I will know why I care, why I yearn for it like a kid pitching his tent under the stars. Maybe the river will let me know why it has become a slow-moving prayer. Maybe driving to the river has taught me it's good to be alone sometimes, if I carry the memory of its rhythm and currents with me wherever I go, the cleansing, quiet knowledge of something greater than myself.